THE COMPLEAT FACILITATOR

A GUIDE

BARRY J. ROBERTS
KEVIN UPTON
AND THE HOWICK ASSOCIATES QI TEAM

MADISON, WISCONSIN

ISBN 0-9646972-0-3

Printed in the United States.

THE PRODUCTION TEAM:
Dick Boelter was the senior art director and designer. Terri Poburka assisted in the graphic design and handled the type and layout. Mary Kessens took on the tasks of production coordinator. Jennifer Winiger provided the final editing and proofreading.

TECHNICAL DETAILS:
Graphic design and layout were done using Quark XPress®3.3 for Macintosh. The dominant body copy typeface is Berkeley, and the headlines are Futura. The paper used for the core of the book is Mountie Matte 100# Text. The cover is on Carolina C1S Cover 18#. Printing, filmwork and assembly were completed at Kramer Printing in Madison.

DEDICATION

In 1653 Izaak Walton published *The Compleat Angler.* Although nominally about fishing, the book is still regarded as the seminal work on the uses of recreation by the people of England. Most reviewers consider the work witty and comprehensive. By selecting the name *The Compleat Facilitator*, we salute Walton and we hope the work is similarly witty and comprehensive. In addition, we think that facilitation skills, though nominally about the team environment, are also essential skills for anyone who wants to or has to lead people in this age.

We dedicate this work to those who struggle daily with the issues of change in the workplace. We join with you in a commitment to teamwork, to a supportive workplace, and to personal development within the context of superior customer service.

"I shall stay him no longer than to wish him a rainy evening to read this following discourse."

— The Compleat Angler

ACKNOWLEDGMENTS

In many ways, this book is the product of thousands of people, people who have attended Howick Associates training programs over the past ten years, people who have critiqued our programs and materials, and people who have worked for us and with us to create and deliver the programs. The idea for The Compleat Facilitator came from client feedback sessions, especially those conducted in 1992 and 1993.

Barry Roberts, more than any other individual, is the parent of this book. He put in the time gathering material, working with outside experts, writing and re-writing, and reviewing drafts. I consider him the "Facilitator" of this book. About a year ago a small team came together in our offices to begin this project. Present were Ann Conzemius, a consultant on our staff who would shortly leave to take the post of Executive Assistant to the Wisconsin Superintendent of Public Instruction, Ann Lindsey, a free lance writer who would make the first effort at pulling together all of our ideas, and Barry, a consultant on our staff and one of our longest term employees.

Nearly forty people who work in human resources and/or in a team environment went out of their way to participate in this project. Let me recognize each of them here. Louise Fosdick, from Home Savings; Janet Shields, Noel Ferry and Pam Beetham, Wisconsin Power & Light; Tim Hallock, St. Mary's Hospital; Kimberly Hollman and Ann McCarville from Rayovac; Mike Rauls and Barbara Waters, Placon; Holly Mercier, DRG Medical; Kathy Zarr, Northwestern Mutual Life; and Bev Bolz, Perry Printing; all offered ideas, material, and support in the early stage of development. Bev later joined our staff and made some mighty contributions to the final stages too.

At about the midway point in development, we took time out for a series of focus group sessions where we shared our ideas and solicited comments. Holly Mercier, Noel Ferry, Louise Fosdick, Tim Hallock and Kimberly Hollman signed up for another few hours of free labor. They were joined by Tom Birrenkott, from General Casualty;

Debbie Fox, State Capital Employees Credit Union; Judy St. Vincent, CUNA; Susan Schneider, Wisconsin Manufacturers and Commerce; Tom Swenson, Madison Metropolitan Schools; Mike Shaw and Dave Lanphear, Wisconsin Department of Transportation; Cindy Schlough, Madison Area Quality Improvement Network; Marsha East and Margaret McWilliams, University of Wisconsin; Dave Birren, Wisconsin Department of Natural Resources; Myrna Casebolt, Wisconsin Department of Health and Social Services; Mary Brody, Pam Stoner, and Tom Gloudeman, Lands' End; Dan Loichinger, Chuck Cleary, and Joni Aeschbach, Wisconsin Power & Light; Jack Nichols, Perry Printing; Phil Ricco, Wisconsin Department of Revenue; and Jean Hansen, Rayovac.

Let me make it clear right here that none of these fine people is responsible for anything that is not right with this book. They each contributed to the final product, but no one should hold them responsible for it. On the other hand, everyone on the staff at Howick Associates does share in the responsibility for the final product. Stuart Daily, LuAnn Felton, Scott Savage, and Wayne Reschke, each took part in the planning and development of the book. Each played a role in editing and reviewing the material as it evolved. Each took on additional work so that others could concentrate on the book.

Finally, I would be remiss if I did not close by thanking Kevin Upton. At various times in this project he served as writer, editor, consultant, production manager, and cheerleader. Me? Mostly I did what I was told to do, paid the bills, and fretted a great deal.

Drew Howick
President
July 1994

TABLE OF CONTENTS

INTRODUCTION

THE COMPLEAT FACILITATOR: A GUIDE

ARE YOU A FACILITATOR? READ ON:

If you're functioning in the role of a facilitator, you've probably gone through some sort of "facilitator training," but months might have passed between your training and your first chance to use what you learned. You may be a manager, or a team leader who wants to develop a facilitating style. Maybe it's been a long time since you've been a facilitator. Maybe you facilitate meetings regularly, but you'd like some more hints on handling teams and the group process.

IF YOU:

Have already had some sort of facilitator training

•

Want to know how your colleagues handle situations

•

Want memory joggers on facilitation techniques

•

Want your fears and concerns addressed

•

Want some fresh ideas and a burst of enthusiasm

THIS BOOK IS FOR YOU!

A FEW DEFINITIONS

Throughout the Facilitator's Guide we use a few terms that can be misunderstood because of ordinary language usage. To keep things simple, here are the definitions that we use.

TEAM:
A group of people working together for a purpose — to accomplish a specific organizational goal. Our definition of team may include project teams and work teams, in addition to management teams, boards of directors, work units, etc. Because each of these teams has a purpose and is functioning to accomplish a goal, each would benefit from teamwork, which is what you, the facilitator, are trying to promote.

TASK:
The goal, mission, or project statement of the team.

TEAM LEADER:
The person with formal authority to direct the team effort, assemble resources for the team, and report the team's decisions and actions. During team meetings, the team leader is an active participant and part of the decision making process. Leaders have ownership in the task and express their opinions and ideas.

SUPERVISOR:
A person with authority to direct and evaluate an employee's job related tasks. As a rule, this authority does not carry over into the team.

FACILITATOR:
As we shall see, this is the person who moves the team along a process using acquired skills and techniques. A facilitator's job is to assist a team in performing as effectively as possible. During meetings, the facilitator should remain neutral and objective. You are not part of the decision making process and you have no ownership in the task.

Having a trained facilitator at team meetings is highly recommended and encouraged. Managers, supervisors, or team leaders who don't have this luxury can still use a facilitative style to maximize team performance. Facilitative skills and techniques from this Guide can be used by anyone responsible for running a meeting.

We recognize that people are often called on to serve as both the team leader and the team facilitator. We recommend that, in these situations, you perform as a leader while using a facilitative style. This Guide may assist you in developing that style.

CHAPTER 1

THE ROLE OF THE FACILITATOR

HOW IS THIS CHAPTER ORGANIZED?

There are five sections, each is presented as a discussion. At the end of the chapter you will find a collection of What If topics, little situations that might seem familiar along with some suggestions for dealing with them.

The sections are:

- Why Have a Team Facilitator?
- What Does It Mean to Be a Facilitator?
- Why Have a Facilitator When There's a Team Leader?
- How Is My Role Similar to the Team Leader's?
- How Is My Role Different from the Team Leader's?
- Facilitator Cautions.

WHAT IF...

- I'm in the middle of a meeting and I don't know where to go next?
- The team asks me to resign as facilitator?
- I have strong feelings about the subject?
- The team leader and I get into a conflict?
- I get nervous?
- I have to be both leader and facilitator?

WHY HAVE A TEAM FACILITATOR?

As your organization moves into a more competitive environment, the ideas and suggestions of all employees become more important. Creating an environment in which employees are free to make their contributions involves helping them acquire new problem-solving and interaction skills. At the top of the list of new skills is teamwork. Teams have proven to be more successful than individuals, over the long haul, in problem solving; in process improvement; in new product development; and in customer service.

Your assignment is vital to the organization because many individuals have little experience working in teams. The workplace has traditionally been focused on individual assignments. Rewards have tended to be individual in nature. But that is all changing. Basically, your job is to teach teamwork.

Your role is objective and impartial. You will have to provide candid feedback on what's going on with the team and offer suggestions that will help turn the group of individuals into an effective team.

When you are successful, the team will learn to function successfully without you.

WHAT DOES IT MEAN TO BE A FACILITATOR?

As a facilitator, you have a different role than other team members. Ideally, you will not be directly affected by the recommendations of the team, and will, therefore, be able to maintain objectivity while guiding the team process.

You will work with the team leader to plan meetings and to plan the team process. You will support the leader by helping to manage meetings, provide feedback, and focus the team's efforts.

Webster's defines "facilitate" as "to make easier." Your job is to make the team's work easier by managing the process and the dynamics.

You will not participate in the work of the team, rather, you support the team in getting its work done. You will support the team by providing structure, tools and feedback on how to accomplish its task, on how to work well as a team, and on how to maximize individual contributions. Through the guidance of the facilitator, an effective team manages the TASK, TEAM, and INDIVIDUAL functions of a team. Keep the following questions in mind when monitoring the team:

FUNCTIONS OF A TEAM

TASK:
- Do we still have our goal, mission, and purpose in sight?
- Are we doing the right things?
- Are we following our meeting agenda?
- Do our discussions stay on topic?
- Are we getting the work done?

TEAM:
- How is the team working together?
- Is everyone involved?
- Are we listening to each other?
- How do we deal with differences of opinion?
- What is the climate among team members?

INDIVIDUAL:
- Do individuals understand their role on the team?
- Are individuals expressing their opinions?
- Are we tapping into the expertise of each individual?
- Do individuals feel comfortable being on the team?
- Do individuals display a positive attitude?

AS A FACILITATOR YOU ARE EXPECTED TO...

- Guide, assist and coach the team.
- Help team members be clear about their roles and responsibilities.
- Identify and remove barriers to effective team dynamics.
- Provide constructive feedback to the team and individuals.
- Provide structured processes and tools to accomplish the team goals.
- Help the team be clear about its purpose.
- Observe, diagnose and aid team performance.
- Create an atmosphere which encourages creative ideas and active input from all team members.
- Keep meetings focused and moving.
- Help the team establish a supportive climate to encourage honest, productive communication.
- Assist the team in dealing with conflict.
- Generate discussion about how to improve team performance.
- Assist the team in problem-solving activities.
- Give the team opportunities to review its own performance.
- Help the team develop the skills to become increasingly self-sufficient.
- Provide feedback to the team leader and team members.

WHY HAVE A FACILITATOR WHEN THERE'S A TEAM LEADER?

The team leader has a stake in the outcome, as a manager or someone affected by the results. This can lead to a lack of objectivity and even reduce trust within the team. Team members tend to defer to team leaders, which can inhibit effective teamwork.

It helps a team to have a facilitator who is an objective, outside resource providing feedback on the process and dynamics taking place. In addition, you have been trained in team dynamics and problem solving skills.

As a facilitator, with no stake in the outcome, you can challenge the team. You can be a resource against the tendency of teams to get trapped in common assumptions and perceptions. You can provide the tools for more creative problem solving.

HOW IS MY ROLE SIMILAR TO THE TEAM LEADER'S?

BOTH TEAM LEADERS AND FACILITATORS:

- Keep the meeting focused and moving.
- Help team members be clear about their task, roles and responsibilities.
- Outline steps the team will use.
- Guide the team in the development of an action plan.
- Effectively manage meetings.
- Balance participation among team members.
- Encourage constructive discussion of controversial issues.

HOW IS MY ROLE DIFFERENT FROM THE TEAM LEADER'S?

FACILITATOR:

- Is objective and impartial.
- Has no vested interest in the task.
- Remains neutral.
- Does not provide input pertaining to content.
- Is not part of the decision making process.
- Monitors the team process.

LEADER:

- Is an active team member.
- Has a vested interest.
- Voices opinions and ideas.
- Provides input.
- Is part of the decision making.
- Represents the team within the organization.
- Gets resources for the team to do its work.

There are some pitfalls that a facilitator should be aware of and try to avoid. Read on.

FACILITATOR CAUTIONS

DON'T TURN THE TEAM OFF

So much is expected of you as a facilitator. Sometimes facilitators cause themselves problems with behavior that turns the team off. Here are a few behaviors that work against you in your facilitator role.

- Showing up unprepared. If you refuse to put in the extra effort, how will you get the team members to act any differently?
- Getting involved in the discussion and monopolizing it. You are supposed to assist the team not take it over.
- Putting people down, cutting them off, getting personal in your remarks. You are there to help the team, guide the team, and keep the team focused on its task.
- Showing that you resent a question by your body language or facial expression. You are supposed to be encouraging questions and participation.
- Letting team discussions develop into battles and arguments. Your job calls for intervention in personal disputes. Step in, restore focus, get the team back on task.

What If?

WHAT IF... I'M THE SUPERVISOR AND I'M FUNCTIONING AS THE TEAM FACILITATOR, WHAT SHOULD I DO?

- State your concern to the team. Discuss how the problem could affect the team dynamics and output.
- Bring in 2 hats. Change them as you change roles.
- Ask for feedback from the team on how well you are handling the dual roles. Let the team guide you.
- Bring in someone else to facilitate. You can serve as the team leader or a key resource person.

WHAT IF...THE PERSON SERVING AS THE TEAM LEADER IS UNCOMFORTABLE IN THAT ROLE?

- Meet with the leader before the session. Agree on an action plan for the meeting. Meet again after the session to discuss what happened and to preplan the next session.
- Talk to the leader. Assess the causes. Depending on the outcome, either change leaders or work on a leadership development plan.
- Rotate the leader role among the participants.

WHAT IF... I'M THE SUPERVISOR, I'M FUNCTIONING AS THE TEAM FACILITATOR AND EVERYONE DEFERS TO ME?

- Clearly state how you see your role as facilitator and discuss how they see the issue affecting them.
- Learn to reflect questions back to the team. "That's a good question, how would the rest of you respond?"
- Don't be the first to contribute ideas or respond to questions. Let others talk first.
- Have a ground rule that your comments will always be last.
- Have a ground rule that "Rank has no privilege."
- Change facilitators. The team is responding to you only as a leader or expert.

WHAT IF... I'M IN THE MIDDLE OF A MEETING AND I DON'T KNOW WHERE TO GO NEXT?

- Review the agenda with the team. Check off the items that have been covered; the decisions that have been made; and the actions that have been taken or recommended. Ask the team for suggestions on the next step.
- Take a break. Consult with the team leader about the next step.
- Adjourn the meeting early.
- Consider the possibility that you have taken the team as far as your skills will allow at this time. Seek additional facilitation resources either within your organization or from outside professionals.

What If? continued

WHAT IF ... I'M PREPARING FOR A MEETING AND I GET NERVOUS?

- Recognize that this is normal.
- Anticipate feeling some anxiety and have a plan to deal with it.
- Learn and use relaxation techniques.
- Practice positive visualization: don't waste energy seeing yourself fail. Visualize success. See yourself doing an effective job of delivering your message with impact.
- Keep the session in proper perspective. Team facilitation is an on-going process. You will have many opportunities to work with the group. Many opportunities to develop a rapport.
- Arrive for meetings early. Arrive prepared.
- Take a moment before you begin for a deep breath, review your agenda, make eye contact with each team member, or do whatever else usually helps you feel more confident and settled.
- Focus on the needs of the team.

WHAT IF... I HAVE STRONG FEELINGS ABOUT THE SUBJECT AND I'M THE TEAM FACILITATOR?

- Alert the team that you have a bias, so they can give you feedback if your values begin to intrude into the team process.
- Play a "devil's advocate" role. Explain what you are doing. Ask someone else to facilitate while you play this role.

VISUALIZE CONFIDENCE

You know what it looks like, you've seen it a hundred times in movies, on stage, and in person.

- Make direct eye contact.
- Make bold gestures.
- Give clear directions.
- Speak with authority.
- Speak at an appropriate volume.

Be confident! Play the part! You wear it well!

CHAPTER 2

MEETING MANAGEMENT

HOW IS THIS CHAPTER ORGANIZED?

This chapter's organization follows the Plan, Do, Study, Act (PDSA) process. This approach will help your meetings be successful.

- **Plan** encompasses meeting logistics: setting objectives and developing an agenda, and preparing participants for the meeting.
- **Do** is the meeting itself: facilitating, record keeping, building open communication, increasing participation, and accomplishing the task.
- **Study** is the step that too many teams leave out. This is an evaluation of the meeting from the participants' perspective with your own insights added as an objective contribution. It is important to evaluate the meeting itself, as well as the results of the meeting — the progress being made on the task.
- **Act** refers to putting the information from Study to use. That is, making improvements for the next meetings.

WHAT IF...
- I can't get everyone together at the same time?
- The key decision makers are on the team, but they don't show up for team meetings?
- The meeting gets off track?
- I'm uncomfortable with the direction the team is taking, even though they're happy?

"Those who fail to plan, plan to fail."

— Ben Franklin

WHY PLAN?

PLANNING:

- Creates a positive first impression of the facilitator.
- Allows you to position the team members in their roles as participants in an effective and dynamic team.
- Motivates team members to attend meetings, to volunteer, and to complete team tasks.
- Removes some of your anxiety and helps you run a smooth meeting.
- Sets the stage for team interaction.
- Encourages team members to participate, have fun and recognize that they can make a significant contribution.
- Ensures that your meetings make the best use of participants' time, talent, and energy.
- Provides a roadmap for the team to follow in accomplishing its task.
- Can be the difference between facilitation that fails and facilitation that succeeds.

TO MEET...OR NOT TO MEET...

On Fortune Magazine's list of the top ten time wasters, meetings rank third.

How often have you heard people complain about meetings during which little, if anything, was accomplished? Not only are these sessions unproductive, they take valuable people away from their jobs for no good reason. The obvious question, then, is why do we continue to have meetings?

Conducted properly, a meeting is one of the best ways to exchange information among a number of people. At the same time, a meeting allows you to check for each individual's level of understanding. This exchange can lead to any or all of several positive outcomes.

OUTCOMES OF A WELL RUN MEETING

- High quality decisions or solutions.
- Effective implementation of strategies.
- Agreement on responsibilities or assignments.
- Generation of new ideas.
- Better understanding of new policies, new procedures, or other changes.
- Collaborative efforts.
- Problem solving.
- A multi-party exchange of information.

Regular meetings, well run regular meetings, will help ensure that the team is making steady progress on the task. There are, however, situations when holding a meeting is neither efficient or a good use of team members' time.

DON'T HOLD A MEETING WHEN...

- You lack a specific agenda.
- Just because it's scheduled.
- Other methods will work better:
  - inter-office memo.
  - meeting privately with individuals.
  - phone conference.
- Organization or production demands take priority.
- You can consolidate your agenda with another meeting.
- A number of team members cannot attend.

OBJECTIVES

Now that you've decided that a meeting is in order, it's time to identify the objectives that need to be accomplished during the meeting. DRAFT CLEAR OBJECTIVES. PUT THEM IN WRITING.

EFFECTIVE OBJECTIVES

- State the desired outcomes or results.
- Can be observed and measured.

AVOID:	To discuss the safety situation in plant C.
INSTEAD:	To identify the cause(s) for the increase in the number of accidents in plant C.
AVOID:	To discuss ways to decrease absenteeism.
INSTEAD:	To identify ten ways to decrease absenteeism.

AGENDA

Once you are sure that a meeting is needed and you have some clear objectives in mind, it is time to draft an agenda.

WHAT'S THE PURPOSE OF AN AGENDA?

An agenda, especially one that is distributed early, gives team members a chance to prepare. It shows them that you value their input and want them to be successful in team meetings. And it says that you want the team to have an effective project result.

A written agenda communicates your meeting plan to participants. By stating the expectations, you greatly increase your chances of conducting a productive, well-managed meeting.

A well-written agenda will:

- Identify the names of the team members.
- Set the time and place of the meeting.
- Inform participants of the order of business.

Agenda
Time
What
Who
Objective
2:00
Check-in
All
Focus
2:10
Decision matrix
Mary
Develop criteria
3:00
Assess options
Juan
Prioritize options
4:00
ID top options
Mary
Build consensus
4:45
Next meeting
George
Set agenda
4:55
Check-out
All
Feedback
Assignments: Bob - research costs of top 3 options

- Specify time to be spent on each item.
- Identify the objectives to be met.
- Inform team members of their pre-meeting responsibilities.
- Identify any guests who might be present.

**CHECK YOUR AGENDA AGAINST YOUR OBJECTIVES.
IS THERE A GOOD MATCH? WILL THE AGENDA HELP YOU
ACCOMPLISH YOUR OBJECTIVES?**

BUILDING AGENDAS FOR THE NEXT TEAM MEETING

Help teams build their own agenda for the next meeting at the end of each meeting. This:

- Builds commitment to the agenda.
- Models the team process.
- Ensures relevant agenda items.
- Increases the probability of assignment completion.

LOGISTICS

- Select a Date and Time based on:
  - Team needs.
  - Meeting objectives.
  - Length of your agenda.
  - Work schedules of team members. (Especially when they are on different shifts.)
  - Organization or production demands.
  - Schedules of guests who need to be in attendance.
  - Availability of meeting space.
- Select a Location based on:
  - Number of participants.
  - Special equipment needs.
  - Ease of access, insure accommodations for handicapped participants.
  - Freedom from interruptions.
  - Anticipated length of meeting.
  - Optimal seating arrangements for the desired interaction.
  - Comfort of participants.

- Other Planning Activities:
  - Reserve required equipment.
  - Order refreshments.
  - Prepare necessary visual aids, handouts, etc.
  - Reserve space.
- Prepare the Participants:
  - Send a copy of the agenda for the meeting to each participant two to five days before the meeting.
  - Send materials to be reviewed in advance allowing sufficient time for them to prepare for their participation. Keep documentation and supporting material brief.

Team members who come prepared are better motivated, produce more, and derive greater satisfaction from the meeting.

"The proof of the pudding is in the eating..."

— Don Quixote de la Mancha
Miguel de Cervantes

Having completed all of the necessary tasks of the planning stage, you are now ready to facilitate a meeting. This is the DO phase of PDSA.

JUST BEFORE THE MEETING...

- Write the agenda on a flip chart sheet and hang it in the meeting room.
  - Make sure the room is arranged properly.
  - Check any special equipment to make certain that it works.
  - Check the placement of any special equipment. Can people see each other and the visual aid?
  - Does the seating arrangement foster the type of discussion and participation that is desired?

Meeting participants have arrived. You are now ready to begin the meeting. Understanding how meetings are organized will assist you in conducting an effective meeting.

A MEETING CONSISTS OF THREE DISTINCT STAGES:

1. The Opening.
2. Accomplishing the Agenda.
3. The Closing.

OPENING THE MEETING

- Start on time.
  - Sets expectations.
  - Shows you intend to stick to the agenda.
  - Rewards team members who are on time.
- Welcome and Introductions.
  - Provides an opportunity to thank everyone for attending.
  - Reminds you to introduce any guests who are present.
- Warm-up ("Ice Breaker") Activity.
  - Stimulates discussion and participation.
  - Releases thoughts about other work and other problems.
- Explain the purpose, importance, and desired outcome of the meeting.
  - Clarifies the expected results of the meeting.
  - Helps focus your discussions.
- Review the Agenda.
  - Determines if there are any additions or changes necessary.
  - Identifies the topics to be covered.
  - Checks on the appropriateness of time allotments.
- Review the Ground Rules.
- Clarify the Roles of the Participants.
  - Record Keeper
  - Time Keeper
  - Team Leader
  - Facilitator
  - Members

ACCOMPLISHING THE AGENDA

- One item at a time.
  - Introduce the item and/or the responsible person.
  - Collect and clarify the relevant information.
    - Cover all known information.
    - Indicate if further information is needed.
    - Identify limitations that may exist.
    - Seek active team participation.
  - Seek suggestions, solutions, alternatives.
    - Encourage team participation.
    - Build on useful suggestions.

- Reach agreement on specific actions.
    - Clarify.
    - Detail responsibilities.
    - Make certain that a team member is accountable for every decision made.
- Summarize the discussion on each agenda item.
- Test for consensus on each item before moving on to the next item on the agenda.
- Spend an appropriate amount of time on each item before moving on.
- Maintain focus throughout the meeting.
  - Stick to the agenda.
  - Create an "Issue Bin" to collect new items that come up and merit discussion at some other time.

THE CLOSING

- Review the accomplishments of the meeting.
- Summarize any decisions that were made.
- Review assignments.
  - What needs to be done?
  - Who will do it?
  - When will it be done?
- Develop an agenda for the next meeting.
- Evaluate the meeting.
  - What went well?
  - What needs improvement?
- Set the time and date for the next meeting.
  - Insure participation by having team members check their calendars.
  - Reinforces the on going nature of the team.
- Thank team members for their input and participation.
- Adjourn.

How To's

ICE BREAKERS

SELF INTRODUCTION

- Members introduce themselves to the group.
- Each member should be told to cover:
  - Name.
  - Department.
  - Position.
  - Length of service.
    (Put these items on a flip chart in advance!)
- Make it more interesting by having each member describe a recent incident related to the team's assignment. Or ask them to explain their reason for participating in the group.

FIRST JOB INTRODUCTION

Have members introduce themselves by giving their name and department. Ask them to talk about their first job, covering the points:

- What was the job?
- What did you do?
- How did you feel in that job?
- How were you treated by your co-workers? By management?
- What did you learn about the "world of work" from that job?
  (Put these items on a flip chart in advance!)

INTRODUCE PARTNERS

- Pair off the group. Ask each person to "interview" their partner. Give them 2 minutes per person for the interviewing (4 minutes total). Have them ask each other questions like:
  - Name.
  - Position in company.
  - Length of time with company.
  - Other jobs they've held.
  - Hobbies.
  - What they hope happens as a result of this team process.
  - How they were selected for the team.
  - Something different, unusual or unique about him/her (that they'd care to reveal).
    (Put these items on a flip chart in advance!)
- Have each person introduce his/her partner to the team.

CIRCULAR WHIP

- Have members introduce themselves.
- Then ask members to respond to a word or simple question. (e.g. "What do customers expect from us?")
- Have a member give his/her brief answer and continue around in a circle.

ICE BREAKERS

SUPERLATIVES

Ask the group members to examine the group silently and decide on a superlative adjective (e.g. youngest, tallest, hairiest, etc.) that describes themselves in reference to the rest of the group.

- Have each person tell his/her adjective.
- Test the accuracy of the perception with the group.

CHECK IN (FOR ON-GOING MEETINGS)

- Ask each participant to say a few words about how they are feeling at that time.
- Feelings can be either work or personal issues.
  (This helps you become aware of what feelings or problems members are bringing to the meeting that may influence participation or motivation.)

HOPES AND CONCERNS

- Have participants identify their hopes for the problem-solving team and their concerns about what may come of it.
- Have the team discuss what it can do to help realize the hopes and prevent the concerns from developing.

NEEDING EACH OTHER

- Ask participants to break into groups of 3 or 4.
- Give each group a form with the letters of the alphabet running down the left side.
- Tell them to wait until you say "Go" and give the following instructions:
- Once you tell them to start, they are to look for an item that begins with each letter of the alphabet. (e.g. Pen for "P," comb for "C," tape for "T," etc.)
- They can use anything they have brought with them, in their pockets, purses or briefcases.
- However, once they've identified an item, they have to lay it on the table in front of them.
- The same item can NOT be used twice.
- You will be timing them. The first group to complete its sheet wins.
- Check over their lists and items.

BUILD A CLIMATE FOR OPEN COMMUNICATION

To communicate openly and honestly, your team members will need:

PERMISSION

Individuals may need permission to bring up an idea or concern, especially if it may cause conflict or tension in the group. Build permission by:

- Announcing, up front, that issues or problems should be brought up for discussion.
- Modeling open and honest communication.
- Providing avenues at meetings to raise concerns in a structured way.

RESPECT

Fear of embarrassment or of being discounted can cause people to keep their thoughts to themselves. Build respect by:

- Listening thoughtfully.
- Valuing all contributions.
- Never allowing others to attack, ridicule, or interrupt.
- Keeping the conversation focused on issues, not individuals.
- Groundrule: no put downs.

INITIATIVE

Individuals need to feel that bringing up a concern or idea will make a difference. Build initiative by:

- Answering questions.
- Asking for group response and input.
- Recording all contributions.
- Asking individuals, by name, for their ideas or opinions.
- Thanking people for their input.
- Following through on issues, suggestions, input.

Telephone Team Minutes

Date: June 12

Present: John W. Debbie M. Chris T. Gary S. Manuel R.

Absent: Mary A.

Key Points/Outcomes:
Decisions:
Assignments:
Next Meeting Date:
Next Meeting Agenda:

DO

ALWAYS RECORD

- Date and time of meeting.
- Names of attendees.
- Agenda items.
- Process/procedures used for each item.
- Main points made in the discussion.
- Action taken, decisions made.
- Assignments to be completed between meetings.
- Items to be carried over to future agendas.
- Agree on how soon after the meeting minutes should be circulated and who should receive them.
- Agree on a standard format so team members will recognize their minutes among other papers on their desks.

How To's

INCREASE PARTICIPATION

- Set participation as the norm.
- Seat team members so they can easily make eye contact with each other.
- Call on people by name.
- Use techniques that get people talking to a partner to generate ideas.
- Ask open-ended questions.
- Learn to feel comfortable with silence — wait for a response.
- Make eye contact with your team members.
- Ask for it.
- Give people time to think of, or write down their ideas before asking that they be shared with the group.
- Contact quiet members between meetings or during breaks — encourage them to participate.
- Acknowledge all responses.
- Summarize and restate key comments/questions.
- Aim questions addressed to the facilitator back to the group.
- Write key statements on a chart.
- Describe to the group what you see occurring.
- Encourage participation.

KEEP THE MEETING MOVING AND FOCUSED

A meeting that keeps moving and stays focused is a meeting that is productive, effective, and fun. Facilitators who keep meetings moving and focused develop good reputations within their organization. Keep it moving and focused by:

GUIDING:

- Observing cues:
  - "there seems to be confusion..."
  - "perhaps it's time to move on..."
  - "we'll continue this next week, when..."
- Clarifying:
  - paraphrase key statements and ideas.
  - clear up obvious confusion.
  - stop the team to check if everyone understands before moving on.
  - "let's see where we are..."
  - "if I understand correctly..."
- Focusing:
  - get back on task.
  - refer to the agenda.
  - visually focus on the flip chart or other visual aid.
  - "to get back to our meeting objectives..."
  - "the point currently under discussion..."
  - create an "issue bin".
- Stimulating:
  - ask open-ended questions.
  - generate ideas.
  - suggest ideas of procedures.
  - "for example, has anyone ever...?"
- Balancing:
  - encourage others to speak.
  - ask individuals for their ideas, use individual names.
  - make eye contact.
  - ask "any other suggestions?"
- Summarizing:
  - review what has been discussed.
  - restate decisions.
  - bring closure to items before moving on.
  - "Jim will follow up on..."

How To's

ISSUE BIN

- Post a sheet of chart paper on the wall labeled "Issue Bin." When issues come up that need to be dealt with later, or in another meeting, have the scribe jot them on the "Issue Bin" page. Review the issues at the end of the meeting; ask which ones have not been addressed. Put those on the agenda for the next meeting, if appropriate. Or pass them on to the appropriate person or team to deal with the issue.
- Post chart paper, title it "Issue Bin," "Parking Lot" or "Side Issues." Place Post-it™ Notes on the tables within reach of participants. As issues occur to the participants, ask them to write them on the Post-its and place the Post-its on the chart.

Issue Bin

* Will there be support for our recommendations?
* What will be the future of our department?
* Why did Joan change jobs?

BUILDING A NEW TEAM

If you are facilitating a newly created team, the emphasis of your initial meetings should be on team building. Developing good working relationships between team members is one of the main ingredients of successful teams. As the facilitator of a new team, you can promote the development of teamwork through the use of "Ice Breakers" and "Ground Rules."

ICE BREAKERS

Ice Breakers are short activities that are generally used at the beginning of a meeting. They can be formal exercises or informal discussions. Ice Breakers serve the following purposes:

- Help participants feel comfortable and relaxed.
- Enable individuals to get to know more about each other.
- Help participants to clear their minds of distractions.
- Get everyone talking and into a participative mood.
- Add humor.
- Set a positive tone for the meeting.

GROUND RULES

Ground Rules are norms or standards of behavior that team members agree to adhere to during team meetings. Once agreed to, they become expected behavior for the team.

DO

SET GROUND RULES/MAKE TEAM AGREEMENTS

- Have the team establish the Ground Rules they're willing to follow and think they need to be productive and successful.
- Begin with a statement such as: "We're going to be working together on an on-going basis. So we don't get "blind-sided" and/or frustrate each other, let's set some ground rules up front to determine how we will work together."
- Setting ground rules will clarify expectations, guide team members in decisions about how to handle difficult situations, and reduce the likelihood that conflict will occur.

Some issues that should be considered when teams begin to establish their own Ground Rules:

- Attendance: A high priority should be placed on meeting attendance. Team members should determine what will be considered legitimate reasons for missing a meeting. Team members should contact a designated person when they cannot attend a meeting. The team should discuss and agree on the number of people who need to be present in order to hold a meeting.
- Promptness: Team meetings should start and end on time.
- Meeting place and time: If possible, determine regular meeting time and location. If schedules don't permit a regular meeting time, discuss how meetings will be scheduled.
- Participation: Team members can discuss and commit to the level of participation they expect from each other. Balanced participation should be encouraged.
- Conversational courtesies: This is a good time for team members to remind each other (or for you to step in and remind the team) of the basics of effective communication in a team — one person speaks at a time, all listen attentively, all are respectful of ideas, etc.
- Assignments: Commitment to completing assignments between team meetings. Sharing of responsibilities should be encouraged.
- Interruptions: Decide when and what kind of interruptions will be tolerated. For example, introduce the "100 mile rule." Imagine that the meeting is being held 100 miles away. Would the interruption be important enough to deal with if you were 100 miles away?
- Rotate routine tasks: The team determines how it would like to rotate responsibilities for routine tasks like taking team records, writing reports,

reserving the room or bringing the donuts! Make sure that no one gets "stuck" or type cast in a single role.

- Confidentiality: Decide what discussion stays in the room versus what information should be communicated and shared.
- Rank/authority: Decide how decisions are going to be made; determine what authority the high-ranking members will have (each member has an equal vote, high-ranking members speak last, etc.)
- Ask for volunteers for functional roles:
  - Leader
  - Timekeeper
  - Recorder*
  - Scribe**

  Benefits:
  - Insures that each function will be done.
  - Gets team members actively involved and feeling like they are contributing positively.
  - You don't become a one-person show.

  * *The Recorder is the person taking notes, to be developed into the meeting minutes later.*

  ** *The Scribe is the team member who records ideas/discussion points/action items on the flip chart or board.*

There can be "role overlap", with one person fulfilling more than one role.

Ground Rules
* Start & end on time
* Respect each other's ideas
* One person talks at a time
* Check your title at the door
* Complete all assignments
* 100 mile rule
* Everyone participates
* Decisions by consensus
* No side conversations

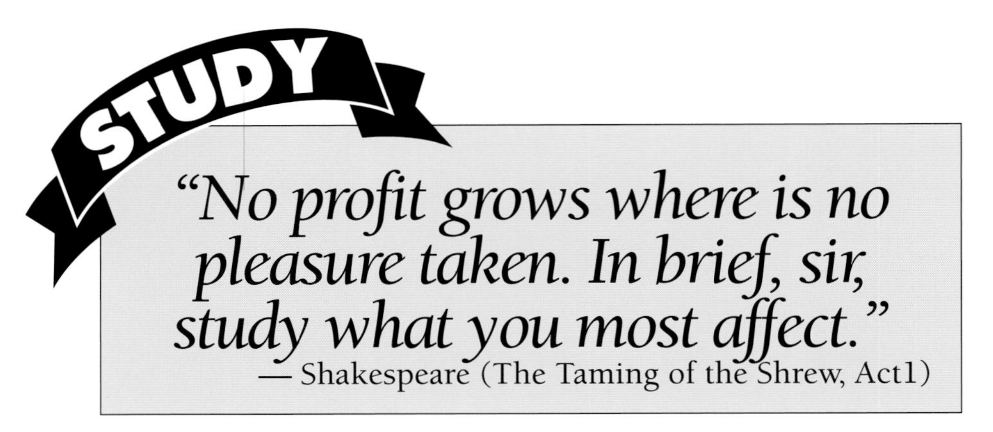

Study is the most ignored aspect of effective meeting management. And, not surprisingly, it's the one step that can take a facilitator from being "pretty good" to being "excellent." Study both the TASK and the TEAM functions.

BENEFITS:

By studying team members' reactions to the meetings you facilitate, you get the feedback you need to be certain that you're serving the needs of the team. Studying the TASK lets you know if the members feel they are making progress on their goal. Studying the TEAM lets you know if the group interaction is fostering cooperation and open communication.

TASK FUNCTIONS:

- Are we accomplishing our task?
- Are we doing the right things?
- Are we following our meeting agenda?
- Do our discussions stay on topic?
- Are we getting the work done?

TEAM FUNCTIONS:

- Is the team working together?
- Is everyone involved?
- Are we listening to each other?
- How do we deal with differences?
- What is the climate among team members?

How To's

MEETING EVALUATION

- Have team members respond to a written evaluation form at the end of the meeting. Share results at the beginning of the next meeting and have the team plan for improvements.
- As facilitator, ask your team for suggestions for improving meeting productivity.
- At the beginning of a team meeting have team members generate three to five performance goals for the meeting. (e.g. Staying on topic, following the agenda, one person speaking at a time, etc.) Half way through the meeting, or at the end, have team members assess performance relative to their goals. Plan for necessary improvements.
- On a rotating basis, assign team members responsibility for observing team performance. Have them share observations with team members. After team members have had an opportunity to respond, plan for necessary improvements.
- Invite in another Facilitator to observe your meeting. Have him/her share observations and feedback. Ask that s/he lead the team in a discussion to plan for improvement.
- Midway through the meeting or at the close of the meeting, ask participants to anonymously write down three words which they would use to describe the meeting. Collect the cards and post the words used. Lead a discussion to plan for improvement.

Meeting Evaluation

Worked Well

* Good agenda
* Everyone participated
* Ended on time
* Met our objectives
* Dealt with conflict in a positive way

Need Improvement

* Room is too hot
* More advance notice of changes in agenda
* Follow through on assignments

In the Act phase, we determine what specific actions need to be built into future meetings, based on the feedback gained in the Study process. Incorporate feedback on both the TEAM and the TASK performance.

Develop action plans for the changes.

- How will the changes be made?
- Who is responsible for making the changes?
- How will you know if the change is successful?

ACT also includes specific activities that need to be performed after the meeting.

- Carry out assignments.
- Record and distribute minutes.
- Discuss specific situations, if necessary, with individual team members.

BENEFITS:

- Continuous improvement as a facilitator.
- Emphasis on the team as your customer.
- Continuous improvement for the team.
- Progress on the task.
- Your own success and satisfaction.

What If?

WHAT IF... I CAN'T GET EVERYONE THERE AT THE SAME TIME?

- Have the team determine a Ground Rule on attendance.
- Change meeting time to meet members' needs.
- Be creative in thinking about alternative meeting times.
- Determine what counts as a quorum.
- Have the team identify the players who are the absolutely critical decision makers; the critical decision makers may change depending upon the situation.
- Decide how decisions will be made, how the team will handle things, procedurally, when critical decision makers are not present.
- Make sure all team members understand what will happen. (e.g. "We'll make a decision with the members who are here." "No decision will be made." or "We will find you and hold you hostage until you agree with our decision.")
- Clarify the priorities of this team vs. other work.
- Challenge team members about their commitment to the team.
- Change team members.

WHAT IF... I CAN'T GET KEY DECISION MAKERS TO PARTICIPATE WITH THE TEAM — THEY'RE NOT AVAILABLE?

- Get to the real reason they're not available. Take appropriate actions.
- Ask the decision makers how they would solve the team task. Will they permit the team to proceed without their input? If yes, have the team draft guidelines (or a "contract") for the decision makers, so everybody is clear on their responsibilities.
- Negotiate "key points" or "milestones" in the decision-making process when the decision makers can meet with the team.
- Make sure the decision makers are aware of the impact of their non-attendance.
- Determine if the project is seen as a priority issue. If not, question whether the team should be formed.

WHAT IF... WE GET INTO POLICY ISSUES THAT ARE BEYOND THE SCOPE OF THE TEAM'S MISSION?

- Review the team's task and objectives and refocus them.
- Ask the team how they want to handle the issue.
- Review the task with management or the steering committee. Determine if they think the team should address these issues.

WHAT IF... THE KEY DECISION MAKERS ARE ON THE TEAM, BUT THEY DON'T SHOW UP FOR TEAM MEETINGS?

- See previous answer on "Getting Everyone to Participate."
- Talk to the decision makers individually, outside of the meeting, to determine why they are not attending. Help them to understand the impact this has on the team. Based on their reaction and response, take appropriate action. Appropriate action may include:
  1. Changing the time and/or location of the meetings.
  2. Asking them to attend specific meetings as needed.
  3. Asking them to serve as a resource.
  4. Question whether the team should be formed.
- Problem solve with the team on how to proceed without key people participating.
- If it is not a priority project, dissolve the team.

WHAT IF... THE MEETING GETS OFF TRACK?

- Summarize the key points discussed and ask the team if the issue is finished or if more time is necessary.
- Draw the members' attention to the appropriate item on the posted agenda.
- Ask someone to be the time keeper and to warn the group when they've used up most of the time allotted to a topic. The team needs to decide if it wants to continue, move on, or have a few members pursue the issue in more detail and report back to the full team.
- Identify the issues that keep coming up; ask the group what they want to do about them.
- If the topic does not need to be addressed, record it in the "Issue Bin."

WHAT IF... I AM UNCOMFORTABLE WITH THE DIRECTION THE TEAM IS GOING IN, EVEN THOUGH THEY'RE HAPPY?

- Discuss your discomfort with the group and remind them of the team project, goals, agenda and scope.
- You need to clarify the direction and re-focus, if necessary.
- Discuss the situation with the Team Leader.
- Discuss the situation with another Facilitator.

What If? continued

WHAT IF... THE KEY DECISION MAKERS ARE ON THE TEAM AND THEY'RE THE ONLY ONES WHO ACTIVELY PARTICIPATE?

- Use other methods to get input:
  - Brainwriting, Round Robin, Affinity, to give everyone a fair chance.
- Talk to decision makers outside of the meeting. Ask them to delay their comments until after others get involved.
- Talk to the decision makers to heighten their awareness of the team dynamics.
- Talk to other team members outside the meeting. Find out why they are not participating. Encourage them to speak up.
- Conduct a team evaluation.
- Ask the "quiet" ones for their ideas during the meeting.

WHAT IF... ABSENT MEMBERS COME BACK TO THE TEAM AND INQUIRE ABOUT PREVIOUS ISSUES AND DECISIONS?

- Offer to discuss their questions after the meeting.
- Make sure everyone gets minutes from previous meetings before the start.
- Create a Ground Rule indicating that, if you are absent, you must get an update from another team member prior to the next meeting.

WHAT IF... THEY FEEL STYMIED BY ISSUES BEYOND THEIR SCOPE?

- Have the team develop potential options and the effects of each option.
- Define who is responsible for the issues that are causing the block. Discuss how each could be removed.
- Seek the assistance of someone who has the necessary skills or expertise to help the team move ahead.
- Examine the membership of the team and decide if a change of members is needed in order to deal with these issues.

WHAT IF... GETTING ALL THE EXPERT INPUT RESULTS IN A HUGE TEAM?

- Divide the team into sub-groups. Have the sub-groups work on parts of the project and have a representative of each sub-group meet with other representatives. Have whole-group meetings only as necessary.
- Bring in experts as guests or ad hoc members when their input is appropriate and needed.
- Re-evaluate the project. It may be too broad. If so, redefine the project.

WHAT IF... THE PARTICIPANTS IN THE MEETING TELL YOU THEY DON'T LIKE HAVING AN AGENDA — IT'S TOO STRUCTURED AND NOBODY FOLLOWS IT ANYWAY. IT'S A WASTE OF TIME TO MAKE ONE UP.

- Discuss the benefits of an agenda.
- Explain the consequences of not using an agenda.
- Suggest they use an agenda for the first two or three meetings. At the end of each meeting, ask them how they thought it went, if they got more accomplished, and if so, why.
- Discuss how agendas are developed and used so that the process can be improved in this team.

WHAT IF... THE FEEDBACK FROM PARTICIPANTS ON ADHERENCE TO THE GROUND RULES IS UNSPECIFIC. WHAT CAN I DO TO HELP THEM BE MORE SPECIFIC?

- Ask them to rate adherence to ground rules on a scale of 1 to 10.
- Ask one member to observe the meeting and report back to the team about what behavior was observed.
- As facilitator, you should also be providing feedback.
- Ask team members for specific examples or quotes.

WHAT IF... THE ONLY GROUND RULES TEAM MEMBERS SUGGEST ARE VAGUE AND UNSPECIFIC, LIKE "BE CONSIDERATE" AND "BE HONEST."

- Ask participants what "Being Honest" looks like/sounds like, and what they have to do to make honesty happen — who's responsible for being honest? What does "honest" mean to you? How do you know when you're being "honest?" Why is it important to be "honest?"
- Ask what behaviors they see as examples of a ground rule. (e.g. What do team members do that shows respect for other people?)
- Share some Ground Rules that have been developed by other teams. Let the team choose the items they want to use.

What If? continued

WHAT IF... THE GROUND RULES ARE ADHERED TO FOR THE FIRST MEETING; ARE REFERRED TO IN THE SECOND; AND ARE NON-EXISTENT BY THE THIRD?

- Have the ground rules printed up on flip-chart sized paper and laminated. Post the chart in the front of the room. At the beginning of each meeting, have someone review them. Ask each participant to pick one and give feedback on adherence to it at the end of the meeting.
- Whenever a Ground Rule is violated, call it to their attention. Refer to the Ground Rules regularly.
- Do a check with the team periodically to determine how well the team is following the Ground Rules.
- Whenever someone violates a Ground Rule, toss a bean bag, or other soft object at them.

WHAT IF... THE GROUP IS WORKING ON ESTABLISHING GOALS FOR THEIR PROJECT, BUT THEY'RE HAVING DIFFICULTY COMING UP WITH THE GOAL?

- Ask "How will we know when we're done?"
- Ask "What are others expecting us to do?"
- Determine where the problem, process, or issue begins and ends.
- Ask "What will be different if we succeed?"
- This may indicate that the project statement is unclear. Get better direction from the Steering Committee or sponsor of the project and/or the team.
- Discuss the project. Team members may have different perceptions. Discuss until a consensus is reached.

WHAT IF... I'M WORKING WITH A PROCESS IMPROVEMENT TEAM. AT THE END OF EACH MEETING (WHICH COINCIDES WITH THEIR NORMAL QUITTING TIME), THEY NEVER WANT TO TAKE THE TIME TO ESTABLISH THE NEXT MEETING DATE?

- Make scheduling of the next two or three meetings the first item on the agenda. Do it at the beginning of the meeting.
- Put "Bring calendars to the meeting" as a "Meeting Preparation" item on the agenda you circulate before the meetings.
- Set aside the last five minutes of each meeting toward setting the next agenda, including date, time and place of the meeting.
- Try to establish a standard meeting time.

WHAT IF... MY PROJECT TEAM HAS TROUBLE STICKING TO THE AGENDA, OR RUNS OVER TIMES ALLOTTED ON EACH ITEM SO THERE ARE ALWAYS ITEMS LEFT OVER AT THE END OF EACH MEETING?

- Review the agenda at the beginning of each meeting. Ask if anyone has modifications. (Things may have come up since the last meeting.)
- Ask participants if the times allocated to each item are appropriate.
- Designate at least one item on the agenda as a FLEX ITEM, so that, if discussions get carried away, the team has already agreed about which item to table until the next meeting.
- Post the agenda on chart paper so that everyone can see it. Refer to the agenda whenever you need to refocus the team.
- Ask the timekeeper to perform "time checks" throughout the meeting. The team then decides whether to continue the discussion, move on to the next item, or assign a few members to work on the topic outside the meeting and report back at the next team meeting.
- Arrange the agenda so that the important items are discussed first. If you run out of time, you can carry over the items to the next meeting or assign someone or some small group to work on the items and report back at the next meeting.

CHAPTER 3

PROBLEM SOLVING

HOW IS THIS CHAPTER ORGANIZED?

The PROBLEM SOLVING chapter is divided into four phases: Problem Definition, Idea Generation, Decision Making and Implementation.

In the **Problem Definition** Section, we'll look at strategies for separating the problem from potential solutions; for probing situations; exposing perceptions; examining the issue statement; and getting to the root cause of a problem.

In the **Idea Generation** Section, we'll look at ways to generate ideas for solutions using techniques designed to get creative input from all participants.

The **Decision Making** Section includes methods for reaching a decision; techniques on the use of a decision matrix; and strategies for building consensus.

Finally, the **Implementation** Section discusses a strategy for successful implementation planning; ways to identify the forces that can influence implementation success; and tips for managing change.

Look for other ways to apply these tools and techniques. Although they are introduced in this chapter, many of these tools and techniques can be used almost any time the teams needs to focus its discussion, make a decision, clarify a problem, or develop an action plan.

Phase One:

PROBLEM DEFINITION

WHY SPEND TIME DEFINING THE PROBLEM?

DEFINING THE PROBLEM HELPS TO:

- Examine the problem objectively.
- Identify the facts and feelings surrounding the problem.
- Identify the key components and players of the problem situation.
- Get involvement from the individuals affected by the problem.
- Challenge common assumptions and perceptions.
- Understand the root cause of the problem so the best long-term solution can be found.
- Prevent "fire fighting" approaches which treat symptoms rather than problems.

AVOID—

Wasting time solving the wrong problem! Do problem definition.

WHAT IS A PROBLEM?

Simply put, it is an undesirable condition. It is usually preceded by several actions or situations that cause the condition. Taking action against the immediate effects may only result in a temporary solution. You may only be treating a symptom. The real problem may not go away. It is important to get at the root cause of the problem or it might not be corrected.

A cause is a condition, or a situation that leads to the problem. A root cause is something that starts a chain reaction of effects or symptoms. If a root cause is eliminated or corrected, the problem will be reduced or eliminated.

Example: Say you have a headache. You may jump right to a short term solution by taking a few aspirin. This is a solution that does not address the underlying problem or cause. To get at the root cause, you need to determine why the headache occurred. Was it because of stress? A lack of sleep? Something you ate? A brain tumor?

Only after knowing the root cause of the headache can you take steps to discover a long term solution that will keep the headache from coming back. The solution might be as simple as taking a nap or as complex as undergoing surgery.

WHAT HAPPENS IN PROBLEM DEFINITION?

THE TEAM NEEDS TO CLARIFY AND DEFINE THE PROBLEM BY ANSWERING QUESTIONS LIKE:

- What do we hope to accomplish by working on this problem?
- What assumptions are we making about the problem?
- What will management, other employees, and our customers be expecting when this problem has been addressed and solved?
- Are there other perceptions of this problem?
- Have we determined the root cause of this problem?
- What additional data/information would help us understand this problem?

HOW TO DEFINE THE PROBLEM:

ASK QUESTIONS:

By asking open-ended questions about the problem you help the team begin the definition process. And you keep the team from jumping to conclusions.

BEGIN BY:

Listing all the questions the team has about the problem. Seek answers to the questions. Gather a broad base of information about the problem.

EXAMPLES:

- Why is this a problem?
- Is this a problem or is it our reaction to this situation that is a problem?
- What is the scope of this problem?
- Who does it affect? In what ways?
- Where can more information be found?
- When did it become a problem?
- Have there been changes in the environment before/when this problem developed?
- What seems to be causing the problem?

There are some additional techniques that can help a team discuss and clarify a problem.

1. IDENTIFYING THE PARTS
List all the identifiable components of the problem (physical resources, people, outside world, professionals, clients, inputs, outputs, time elements, etc.). Study the role each part plays in the problem.

2. EXPANDING THE DATA
Make a list of everything you know about the problem.

3. IDENTIFYING KEY WORDS
Have each team member prepare a statement on what they believe to be important about the problem, including a description of their objectives and concerns.

- Circle the common words or phrases which appear in the statements.
- Give team members a clean copy of the statements and put the common words and phrases on the flip chart.
- Using only those key words or phrases, work as a team to write a new problem statement.

4. EXPOSING PERCEPTIONS
Separate team members into smaller groups representing the views of different stakeholders. Have the groups define the problem from this perspective. Bring the definitions together for discussion/debate. Critically examine the underlying assumptions, implications, and possible consequences of the different definitions.

Problem Statements should reflect what's wrong with the status quo. They should not imply solutions. Effective problem statements:

- Address customer needs.
- Do not imply a solution.
- Represent the problem and its causes at its deepest known level.

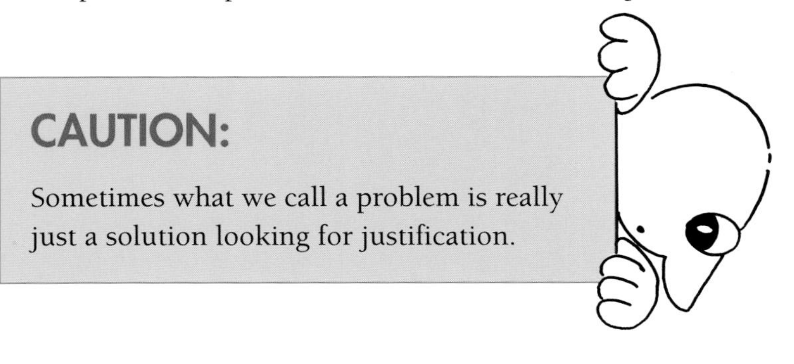

PROBLEM DEFINITION: A PARABLE OF A FLAT TIRE

A man was driving down a rustic country road when, suddenly, his car blew a tire. His quick reaction enabled him to keep the car under control as it swerved on the gravel and sand. He slowed it to a stop. Looking at the steep roadside ditches, he realized that things might have been worse. He might have spun out of control and flipped into a ditch.

With a deep sigh, he surveyed the scene. He was miles from town, there were no farm homes in view, there was no sign of activity in any of the nearby fields, it was hot, and he had a flat. Sighing, again, he removed his jacket, opened the trunk, removed the spare tire, the tire iron and lug wrench, and set about changing the tire. It was at this point that he realized that the jack was missing.

The man engaged in problem definition. The problem is, he told himself, that I have to jack-up the car in order to change the flat tire. Without a jack the job cannot be done, he told himself. He resolved to set out on foot toward the nearest town to find a jack. This, he believed, was the only solution to the problem.

After a walk of about five miles, he reached a service station on the outskirts of town. A helpful attendant offered to drive him back to his car and help him change the tire. To pass the time the man told the attendant about his afternoon of decision-making. After listening a bit, the attendant said, "I could of saved you the walk."

"How could you have done that?" the man asked irritatedly.

"By defining the problem differently," the attendant replied.

Too exhausted from his long, hot walk, the man asked the attendant to explain.

"You thought that the issue was the missing jack because you defined the problem as a need to jack-up the car," the attendant began. "Me, I would of defined the problem as a need to change the tire."

"I don't see the difference," said the man.

"Watch," came the answer.

With that the attendant began to walk slowly, his eyes casting about the sides of the road. Once he stopped to pick up a discarded beer can. Next he grabbed some stones from the side of a field. He brought these back to the car. Then he walked quickly to a pile of field refuse near the end of a plow row and disengaged a sizeable tree stump that had been unceremoniously dumped there. This, too, was placed near the car. Finally, he began to work.

Stones were wedged under the front tires to prevent rolling. Grabbing the rear bumper in both hands, the attendant raised the back of the car ever so slightly, then using his foot, he dragged the tree stump closer and closer until he was able to use his leg to force the stump under the raised rear end. With just a bit more effort, and another lift, the attendant was able to move his new prop closer to the side of the car with the flat tire.

Working steadily but not hurriedly, the attendant next removed the flat tire. The task was now simple because the car, with the front end wedged with stones, did not move when he leaned into the lug nuts. The flat slid off the axle with ease because the car was now held at a stable height.

The man was impressed by the attendant's actions but still didn't see how he was going to complete the change. After all, removing the flat was only half the challenge. So he was genuinely surprised by what came next.

The attendant moved the flat off to the side and then sat down on the road. Reaching for the beer can, he flattened it and began to use it as a shovel. Within a few minutes he had worked enough sand and gravel loose from beneath the dangling axle to allow the spare tire to fit. Then he quickly remounted the lugs, threw the flat and lug tool in the trunk, slammed it shut, and proceeded to kick the stones from against the front tires.

Turning to the man the attendant said, "Follow me back to the station and I'll fix that flat for ya."

"I don't get it," the man offered weakly.

"Don't get what?" asked the attendant.

"How did you know what to do?" came the response.

"It's all in the problem definition," the attendant said after thinking for a moment. "You saw the problem as one of needing a jack, I saw it as needing to change a tire."

Then he added, "Plus, I hate to walk on a hot day."

MORAL:

How you define a problem will affect the solutions to be considered. Time spent in Problem Definition will pay off with more creative options and ultimately, a better solution.

GETTING AT ROOT CAUSES

A favorite technique of problem definition experts is called "Asking 'Why?' 5 Times." This is a technique that allows the team to get beyond the surface symptoms or apparent solutions to reveal the root cause. By repeatedly asking "Why did that happen?" or "Why is that a problem?" the team can determine the causes of the current situation or problem.

EXAMPLE:

1. **Why did the machine stop?**
   Because the fuse blew due to an overload.
2. **Why was there an overload?**
   Because the bearing lubrication was inadequate.
3. **Why was the lubrication inadequate?**
   Because the lubrication pump was not functioning right.
4. **Why wasn't the lubricating pump working right?**
   Because the pump axle was worn out.
5. **Why was it worn out?**
   Because sludge got in.
6. **Why...**

— *Taiici Ohno*
Former Toyota Motor Vice President

A FINAL WORD ON PROBLEM DEFINITION

KEEP IN MIND:

- Poor definition of a problem can inhibit and delay finding the best solution.
- The way you define a problem will influence the solutions you seek.
- Different people within an organization will see the same problem in different ways.
- Clarifying the team's definition of the problem is an important phase of the problem-solving process. It warrants a sufficient allocation of time and energy.
- Verify the team's definition of the problem with individuals affected by the problem in the "real world."
- Collect data and information that will help you understand the situation and the root causes of the problem.
- Remember: If you don't define a problem well, you will probably get to a quick and insufficient solution. Take aspirin for a headache, and the headache may reoccur. But, if you define the problem well, you can correct the root causes and stop the pain.

IDEA GENERATION

The goal of idea generation is to produce as many high quality ideas as possible for solutions to a particular problem.

WHY TAKE THE TIME TO GENERATE SO MANY IDEAS?

Generating ideas will help team members break out of old thinking patterns, develop multiple options, look at all possible ways of reaching a solution and draw potential solutions from a variety of sources.

WHAT OPTIONS ARE THERE FOR IDEA GENERATION?

There are four basic idea generation techniques discussed in this section:

- Brainstorming
- Brainwriting
- Forced Relationships
- Affinity Process

In general, problem-solving is more effective if teams do not always rely on the same idea generation technique. Variety in the process of idea generation will often inspire the team to more ideas.

HOW SHOULD THESE TECHNIQUES BE USED?

Idea generation meetings can either be very free-wheeling or very structured. The style you choose will depend upon the dynamics of the team, the number of people involved, and the type of problem being examined.

BRAINSTORMING

The category of brainstorming refers to techniques which rely on a verbal generation of ideas by the team.

Brainstorming is good to use when:

- The team is small.
- The style of the team is open and participative.
- Team members need to discuss ideas.
- Uniqueness of ideas is important.
- A large number of ideas are needed quickly.
- The problem can be stated simply or broken into parts.
- Members feel free to express themselves.

OBSTACLES TO SUCCESSFUL BRAINSTORMING:

- Personality differences among team members that cause some to talk a lot and others not at all.
- Team members who are very conscious of position or status differences in the group.
- Individuals are inhibited or afraid of appearing foolish.
- The free-wheeling has been difficult to control in the past.
- Team members have found it difficult to defer judging ideas in the past.
- Some team members tend to monopolize discussions.

BRAINSTORMING

Prior to the brainstorming session:

- Develop a statement of the problem.
- If possible, give advanced notice that the team will be brainstorming for possible solutions to the problem.

DURING THE SESSION:

1. Begin the meeting with a review of brainstorming and establish the four rules of brainstorming.
   The Ground Rules:
   a. Criticism or judgment of ideas is deferred until after idea generation.
   b. Free-wheeling is welcomed. All ideas are worthwhile and encouraged.
   c. Quantity is desired. The more ideas generated, the greater the odds that a successful solution will be found.
   d. Combination and improvement on the ideas of others is a good practice. It can produce more creative ideas.
2. Write the problem statement on a board or a flip chart that is visible to everyone on the team.
3. You will usually act as "recorder" to write down all the ideas generated. Use the flip chart.
4. Set an approximate time frame for idea generation. Usually 15 - 30 minutes works best in team meetings.
   Tip: If the issue is complex or challenging in some way, it might work best if you give the team members 5 minutes to write down their ideas individually before beginning the open session.
5. Continue brainstorming for the allotted time. Don't be afraid of lulls. Often a team will get more creative after a lull. Don't end the brainstorming prematurely.
   Adaptation: Try a "round-robin" recording of ideas instead of a free-wheeling session. In a round-robin session, you go around the table seeking ideas from one person at a time. Continue around until there are no ideas left. Team members can pass if they can't think of something when it's their turn. Be certain to enforce a "no-speaking-out-of-turn" rule. The round-robin is more structured and can lead to a more balanced participation by reducing the prospects for domination by a few people.

BRAINWRITING

Brainwriting refers to techniques which rely on silent generation of ideas through writing.

BRAINWRITING IS BEST TO USE WHEN:

- The team is small.
- Status differences need to be equalized.
- There is no need for verbal interaction.
- Team members may be in conflict with each other.
- Quiet members need to be drawn into participation.

OBSTACLES TO SUCCESSFUL BRAINWRITING:

- Team members must be literate and comfortable expressing their ideas in writing.
- Spontaneity and synergy are low during the writing time.
- The lists need to be consolidated and edited to remove redundant ideas.
- People talking will disrupt the thinking of other team members.

THE KEY BENEFIT OF BRAINWRITING:

Some people can't think well in a group brainstorming session. They find the verbal intensity too distracting. Brainwriting allows team members to think through their ideas and to work at their own pace without the pressure of competing to be heard.

How To's

BRAINWRITING

1. Review the process and the ground rules with the team.
   The Ground Rules:
   a. Work silently.
   b. All ideas are worthwhile and valuable.
   c. Write legibly so others can read what you have to say.
   d. Keep it moving. Don't get stuck on one thought.
2. Present the problem statement to the team.
3. The team members write down their ideas on a sheet of paper.
4. As soon as an individual has listed an idea, place the sheet in the middle of the table and exchange it for another sheet. Call it the "Idea Pool."
5. Participants continue to add one idea to the sheets taken from the pool, exchanging them for a new sheet after each additional idea. A team member can use the same sheet more than once. Members can build on the ideas already on the sheet or add entirely new thoughts.
6. Set an approximate time frame for idea generation. Usually 15 - 30 minutes works best in team meetings.
7. Collect the sheets and consolidate all the ideas into one document or onto a flip chart. Once this is done, the team can begin to evaluate the ideas.

FORCED RELATIONSHIPS:

The Forced Relationships technique relies upon forcing together two or more objects, products or ideas. The elements that are combined may be related or unrelated to one another. At least one of the ideas should be directly related to the problem or issue under discussion. The second idea may be related or it could be totally unrelated and used to stimulate creativity.

FORCED RELATIONSHIPS IS BEST TO USE WHEN:

- There seem to be two major ideas but few alternatives.
- Integration of several ideas to form a single solution is preferred.
- You need a creative stimulus.

OBSTACLES TO SUCCESSFUL FORCED RELATIONSHIPS:

- Members hold onto an assumption that there is no way to combine the ideas.
- The outcome is unpredictable. Sometimes you generate great ideas: Sometimes the team can't get into the process.

How To's

FORCED RELATIONSHIPS FOR STIMULATING CREATIVITY

1. Review the process and the ground rules with the team. The Ground Rules:
   a. No judging.
   b. All ideas, even wild or whacky ideas, are desirable.
   c. Don't let assumptions limit your creativity.
2. State the problem.
3. Ask team members to generate ideas in writing individually.
4. Select two team members to read one each of their ideas.
5. Have a third member read another idea. Then, have the team attempt to integrate all three ideas into a single solution.
6. Continue this process until all of the ideas have been read and attempts have been made to integrate them all.
7. Terminate the procedure at the end of the predetermined time period or when all ideas have been heard and combined.

How To's

FORCED RELATIONSHIPS FOR MANAGING CONFLICTING IDEAS

1. Review the process and the ground rules with the team. The Ground Rules:
   a. No judging.
   b. All ideas, even wild or whacky ideas, are desirable.
   c. Don't let assumptions limit your creativity.
2. State the conflicting ideas and write them at the top of a flip chart.
3. Ask the team to brainstorm ways of combining these two ideas into a set of new ideas.
4. Continue this process until the end of the designated time period.

AFFINITY PROCESS

The Affinity Process is a way for the team to generate ideas and to "clump" issues or themes together. Because the process involves both verbal and non-verbal steps, it is a way for the team to create some synergy and creativity and to deal with, what may be, emotionally charged issues. The Affinity Process works best in small teams.

The Affinity Process combines both idea generation and the beginning of decision making because the team has to reach agreement on the organization of ideas. This process can also be used to organize comments or complaints from customers, to collect ideas from non-team members, or to identify causes of a problem.

How To's

AFFINITY PROCESS

1. Phrase the issue or question clearly to the team. Establish the ground rules.
   The Ground Rules:
   - Part of the session will be done in silence.
   - No one-word cards. No cliches.
   - Avoid ambiguous words or phrases.
2. Ask the team members to write their ideas on large (4 x 6) Post-it™ Notes or cards. Ask them to print in clear, large letters using felt tip pens.
3. Ask participants to put their Post-its on the wall or lay their cards on the table randomly.
4. Ask team members to silently sort the cards or Post-its into what they see as related groupings. Anyone may regroup a card if s/he feels it is in the wrong category.
   Tip: If one card keeps getting moved around, you can write a duplicate card so that the idea can be in two places. End this step when the team seems to be settled on most of the groupings. This usually takes about ten minutes.
5. Begin the discussion of the clusters with the team.
   - Sort any ungrouped cards through discussion.
   - Consolidate duplicate cards.
   - Identify a theme for each cluster.
6. Create header cards for each group. Keep the number of headers in the range of 5-10 groups.
7. If any single cluster seems much larger than the others, have the team divide it into sub-headings.

AFFINITY PROCESS IS BEST TO USE WHEN:

- You want a structured idea generation approach to balance participation.
- The team is small.
- You want the team to see the similarity in their ideas so that they can begin consensus building.
- You anticipate generating many ideas. Organizing these ideas into categories or themes will be helpful at the Decision Making phase.

OBSTACLES TO SUCCESSFUL AFFINITY PROCESSES:

- Talking during the silent idea generation or idea organization period.
- Too few ideas are generated.
- The team is too large, more than 10 members, for equal participation.

How To's

STIMULATE CREATIVITY

1. Ask team members for their wildest idea. Make sure that the wildest ideas are voiced and recorded.
2. Give the team a visual stimulus. Show a series of pictures, slides, posters, or physical objects during the idea generation session. The visual stimulus does not have to be related to the problem at all.
3. Ask team members to think from another perspective, or role play. What would a customer say about the problem? What would the CFO say? How would a television newscaster report the problem?
4. Play music while they generate ideas. Any kind of music. Loud or soft, classical or contemporary, rock or country, blues or jazz. Music often stimulates other creative processes.
5. Set time limits but keep pushing until all the time allotted is used. Don't be afraid of lulls in the action.
6. Ask team members to keep notes on ideas they get between meetings. Have them ask non-team members for comments and suggestions. Ask for reports at the next meeting.

A FINAL WORD ON IDEA GENERATION

REMEMBER

- Always review the ground rules.
- Remind team members of the ground rules as needed.
- Use verbal cues. ("What else?" "Say more.")
- Challenge the team. ("Fill the page." "Ten more." etc.)
- Post the pages. Keep all ideas in front of the group.
- Avoid making comments or evaluations, good or bad, during the idea generation period.
- Get input from all team members.
- Check for clarity and common understanding by paraphrasing when necessary.
- Do not contribute ideas. Your job is to manage the process and record the results.
- Review for duplication and understanding before moving on to decision making.
- Look for other opportunities to use idea generation techniques. Try them in weighing the pros and cons of an issue. Or, try them in evaluating action steps. Good techniques are rarely limited to a single application.

Once team members have grappled with the problem statement and generated multiple ideas for potential solutions, it is time to help them reach a decision on which idea to recommend. It is important to note that decision making calls for greater formality than the previous phases of Problem Solving. At this point, the time for free wheeling has come to an end. There are, however, a number of techniques that you can use to help the team through the process.

Phase Three:

DECISION MAKING

WHY STRUCTURE DECISION MAKING?

USING A STRUCTURED DECISION MAKING PROCESS HELPS YOUR TEAM TO:

- Make choices from available options.
- Use objective measures in considering the various alternatives.
- Reach a consensus decision within the team.
- Minimize personal whims as the basis for a decision.
- Focus on how an idea might be made to work as well as recognizing what is wrong with the idea.
- Help the team understand its rationale for the decision.
- Make it easier for the team to communicate its decision.

USING STRUCTURED DECISION MAKING WILL KEEP YOUR TEAM FROM:

- Retreating to old ideas because they are comfortably familiar.
- Jumping to a popular decision without considering all the options.
- Having too many ideas to handle.
- Feeling overwhelmed by the details associated with any solution alternative.
- Forcing an inappropriate decision because of time pressures.
- Having irreconcilable differences regarding alternatives.

MULTI-VOTING

Multi-voting is a way to conduct a poll or a vote to select the most important or popular items from a list of items with a minimum amount of discussion.

Multi-voting typically is done following a brainstorming or brainwriting session.

It works best when you need to reduce a long list of ideas to a short list for in-depth discussion.

It is done through a series of votes, each cutting the list significantly. Even a large list of 50 items can be reduced to a workable number in 2 or 3 votes.

How To's

MULTI-VOTING

1. After brainstorming, brainwriting or any other creative idea generation technique, list the potential solutions on a flip chart or board.
2. Number each item.
3. Have the team review the list. If two or more items seem very similar, combine them, but only if the team agrees that they are the same. Don't let the team get bogged down in this exercise. If it is not clear that items can be combined, leave them alone and proceed with the vote.
4. Have the team members "vote" for several items by writing down the numbers of these items on a sheet of paper in front of them.

   Each team member is allowed to vote for items equal to approximately one-third of the total number of items on the list. (60 items = 20 choices, 38 items = 13 choices, etc.)
5. Tally the votes. This can be done by:
   - Allowing team members to come up and mark their votes next to the items using checks or hash marks. (This is also a way to get people moving in the meeting.)
   - By asking for a show of hands as you go through the list.
   - If there is a need for anonymity, collect ballots and record the votes during a break or between sessions.
6. Cross out the items receiving the fewest votes.

   Ask the team to help you determine the cutoff number of votes. Don't try to reduce the list in one round if you have more than 15 items.
7. Repeat steps 4, 5 and 6 with the remaining items on the list. Remember to adjust the number of votes allowed each team member to one-third of the items remaining on the list.
8. Continue this process until only a manageable number, 7 or fewer items, remains.
9. Have the team discuss the remaining items. Switch to a Decision Matrix technique to achieve a final decision.

DECISION MATRIX

The decision matrix is a technique to assist teams in objectively evaluating alternative ideas.

It is most often used to force the team to seriously consider all the major ideas and when the final selection among alternatives is particularly complex.

WHY USE A DECISION MATRIX?

Most often, when making a decision, no single perfect solution exists. Options A, B and C might meet some of the criteria, while options D and E might meet other criteria, but not those met by options A, B and C.

By listing the options and matching them against the criteria on a chart, you'll be able to clearly see which option meets most of the criteria.

How To's

DECISION MATRIX

1. Draw a matrix on the flip chart.
2. List the options/ideas in any order down the left side of the matrix.
3. List the criteria for evaluation across the top of the matrix.

   Option: Ask the team to assign a weight to each criterion that reflects its relative importance. For example: 1 = low importance, 2 = moderate importance, etc.
4. Rate each option/idea against the criteria. Use a 0 - 5 scale with 5 meaning that the idea meets the criteria totally, and 0 meaning that the idea doesn't meet the criteria at all. Determine ratings by team consensus.
5. Multiply the rating and weighting scores. Place the number in the corresponding boxes in the matrix.
6. Add up the weighted ratings and place the total in the final column headed "Total Weighted Rating."
7. Discuss the high ranking ideas to reach consensus on which is the best solution. The matrix is a tool that helps build consensus. Don't automatically adopt the highest score. Discuss the high ranking alternatives.

Decision Matrix

Decision Criteria

Weighting: Ideas	Low Cost (3) Rating	Low Cost (3) Weighted Score	Customer Assistance (5) Rating	Customer Assistance (5) Weighted Score	Within Timeline (2) Rating	Within Timeline (2) Weighted Score	Total
New telephone system	0	0	3	15	1	2	17
Hire receptionist	1	3	5	25	5	10	38
Answering service	3	9	0	0	5	10	19
New schedule	5	15	2	10	2	4	29
Voice response system	0	0	3	15	4	8	23
Increase of lines	1	3	2	10	3	6	19
Rotate staff coverage	2	6	3	15	2	4	25
Change ad copy to reduce calls	5	15	5	25	5	10	50

BUILDING CONSENSUS

WHAT IS IT?

Consensus is reaching a decision that every member of the team agrees to support.

WHY BUILD CONSENSUS?

A consensus decision is one that all team members will support. Through consensus building, team members will be motivated to work for the implementation of the decision instead of withdrawing support or sabotaging the decision. Members will search for alternatives and will seek clarity on the issues.

Consensus does not necessarily mean that all members are in full agreement or are completely satisfied. It does, however, mean that each team member can honestly say,

- "I believe you understand my point of view."
- "I believe I understand your point of view."
- "I may prefer to do it another way, but I will support this as the team's decision because it was reached in an open and fair manner."

CONSENSUS BUILDING HINTS

- Don't force team members to give in just to avoid conflict. This may result in a "false consensus" where you assume people support the decision but they really don't.
- Seek ways to combine different points and different positions.
- Have those with official authority defer until last before stating their opinions.
- Schedule enough time. Consensus cannot be rushed.
- Avoid reducing the decision to a vote or a coin toss.
- Encourage everyone to participate.

How To's

BUILDING CONSENSUS

- Summarize the team's work up to this point. Clarify the issue and review the options.
- Identify points of agreement.
- Identify points of disagreement.
- Listen carefully to everyone's point of view and their rationale.
- Make sure the team sticks to the Ground Rules during all discussions.
- Determine the underlying assumptions and discuss the validity of those assumptions.
- Obtain additional data, if necessary, to validate those assumptions.
- Challenge perspectives and assumptions.
- Use the techniques and tools (multi-voting, decision matrix, forced relationships) to help the team develop the best solution.

Phase Four:

IMPLEMENTATION

WHAT IS IT?

It is planning action steps, guiding and monitoring the action. It's communicating with those who are affected by or are actually doing the implementation. It's getting feedback for further improvements.

WHY DO IMPLEMENTATION?

There is no point in doing problem solving unless the organization intends to attempt to implement the team's solution.

MOST OF IMPLEMENTATION IS THE UP-FRONT WORK: PLANNING!

HOW DOES IMPLEMENTATION WORK?

Planning is the single most important component of successful implementation. A thorough planning process will consider the following:

ACCEPTANCE:
Will this solution be accepted by the necessary parties, including authority figures and those who will be called upon to make it work? (Note: Acceptance can often be built in to the team by involving those who will be expected to do the implementation in the problem-solving process and in reaching consensus.)

RESOURCES:
What resources (money, people, time, etc.) will the organization need? Are there alternatives?

TIMELINES:
In what sequence should events occur? What is the best schedule? How can it be enforced? Would implementation best occur at a particular time of the year, month, week?

COMMUNICATION:
How will this idea be communicated to others? How will we receive feedback? What questions or concerns might people have? How will we keep the lines of communication open and functioning?

CONTINGENCIES:
How will the organization respond to problems with the implementation plan? Should the team propose a back-up plan? Are there any "safety valves" built into the plan? Is there a way to pre-test the solution?

MOMENTUM:
What will keep the implementation effort going? What if participants become discouraged? How can the organization keep people motivated? How can the team plan for follow-through? How can these ideas be kept viable?

CONTINUITY:
What is the team's role after the problem solution is implemented? Disband? Monitor? Participate in the implementation?

How To's

FORCE FIELD ANALYSIS

Force Field Analysis is a visual listing of possible forces driving or obstructing change.

A Force Field Analysis is useful if a team wants to find out what is (or probably will be) driving, slowing or stopping change from happening.

Force Field Analysis is usually represented in the following way:

Take 10 to 15 minutes for each column and brainstorm as many ideas as you can. (As with all brainstorming, go for quantity. You can clean up the list later.)

Once the team has identified the driving forces and the restraining forces, you can proceed to identify ways to strengthen the driving forces and ways to deal with the restraining ones.

One way to deal with the restraining forces is to do a Contingency Diagram.

How To's

CONTINGENCY DIAGRAM

A Contingency Diagram is a technique for analyzing and counteracting the restraining forces.

1. After doing a Force Field Analysis, select the restraining forces that are (or are going to be) very difficult to overcome.
2. Brainstorm a list of ways to make the undesired state happen. Write these ways on a Contingency Diagram.
3. Then determine what the team must do to prevent these things from happening. Now you know what action must be taken.

Do an action plan based on these strategies.

Force Field Analysis

Driving Forces

* Changing customer needs
* Top management
* Need to reduce costs
* Team involvement in planning

Restraining Forces

* Staff resistance to change
* Cost of new equipment
* Concern for quality

How To's

TROLL SEARCH

Trolls are the fears and restraining forces that "come out from under the bridge" and gobble up the project. As a facilitator, you may need to lead a Troll Search from time to time to be certain that fears are not restraining participation.

Force Field Analysis or Contingency Diagraming can be used as Troll Search techniques. This can be repeated several times over the life of a project. In fact, it would be beneficial to do one at the start of a project, to be sure things and people that should have been included are.

1. Brainstorm all the "fears" (things that could go wrong). Continue the brainstorming session until the team members run out of ideas.
2. On a 0 - 10 scale, calculate both the likelihood of each fear happening, and the severity of it if it did happen.
   Likelihood: 10 means that it has happened, or will. 0 indicates that there is no possibility of it happening. Severity: 10 means that the whole project would crash (and maybe the team members as well). 0 equals no impact at all.
3. Assign one or more "Trolls" to each member to handle. Determine a prevention or contingency plan.
4. At regular intervals, review the "Trolls" to see which ones have been eliminated, which ones still need attention and determine if there are new ones.

(Thanks to Kimberly Hollman, Rayovac)

SUMMARY: PROBLEM SOLVING

For any team to effectively problem solve, it must work through the four phases: Problem Definition, Idea Generation, Decision Making, and Implementation.

As facilitator, your job is to help the team complete each phase successfully before moving on to the next phase. If the team jumps ahead, or skips a phase, conflict or poor decisions may be the result.

Use the techniques and tools presented here to provide variety in meetings. Variety will help you to keep the team members interested and motivated. Interested and motivated people will work toward a resolution of the problem at hand.

CHAPTER 4

DEALING WITH PEOPLE

INTRODUCTION

We've all heard the joke. "If it weren't for the (customers/patients/clients/employees) this wouldn't be a bad place to work."

The truth is, it's the people we interact with who make the world interesting. Sometimes more interesting than we want it to be.

When it comes to facilitating, we are often challenged by the behaviors of people working on teams and in meetings.

This chapter covers the more common difficult behaviors that you might confront in a team setting and offers some suggestions for dealing with them.

HOW IS THIS CHAPTER ORGANIZED?

We'll start the chapter by looking at the stages of team development, offering insights about what the different stages look and sound like, and suggesting what your role is at each stage.

Next, we will examine the difficult behaviors that you will face and we will offer suggestions for handling these behaviors.

We'll move on to looking at ways to give and receive feedback.

Finally, we'll look at strategies for dealing with conflict on a team.

STAGES OF TEAM DEVELOPMENT[1]

Teams naturally grow and change as people work together. Research and long experience show that there are some common stages of team development.

THE STAGES OF TEAM DEVELOPMENT

FORMING
STORMING
NORMING
PERFORMING
ADJOURNING

One-size-fits-all facilitation does not work as the team evolves. Facilitators need to be flexible as the team works through different stages. Get out of sync with the team and you might face conflict or apathy from the team members.

Remember: Your job is to serve the team. You must understand the team and its needs if you are to provide the best service possible as a facilitator.

FORMING

The forming stage occurs as a team begins. This is the time for getting to know each other and for feeling out the situation. It can seem like the first hour at a party or other social gathering. People are polite, they make introductions, and they engage in light chit-chat.

WHAT'S HAPPENING?

- Orientation — to each other, to the purpose of being together.
- Exploring — relationships.

1. Tuckman, B.W. "Developmental sequence in small groups." *The Psychological Bulletin*, 1965, 63, 384-399.

WHAT DOES IT LOOK AND FEEL LIKE?

- Polite!
- Superficial.
- Tentative.
- Concerns about levels of involvement and dependence.
- Concerns about purpose of team.
- Uncertainty about roles, abilities, status.
- Dependence on the facilitator/ leader.
- Little or no risk-taking.
- Suspicion, fear, or anxiety about the team, the task or the people.
- Or, excitement, anticipation, and optimism.

WHAT SHOULD YOU DO?

- Use Ice Breakers and other team building activities to facilitate the forming of the team.
- Ask team members to introduce themselves and say why they are on the team.
- Encourage free expression.
- Model desired behavior, be friendly, express ideas and opinions.
- Ensure open participation in goal setting, ground rule writing, the division of tasks, etc.
- Help the team clarify its purpose and the roles of the members. Consider inviting a guest who can discuss the team's assignment or task. Often this is the manager or a representative of the steering committee that organized the team.

STORMING

Teams move into the storming stage as people develop an understanding of how the team will operate and how individuals will act. The storming represents conflict, confusion, or frustration that occurs in the team. It may occur due to value differences, differing opinions on the project or task, or because of personality or role conflicts that need to get worked out.

WHAT'S HAPPENING?

- Confusion and disagreement about the task and the best way to proceed.
- Ideas are criticized, speakers are interrupted. Behaviors may become rude. Members become argumentative.
- Disputes occur over procedures.
- Cliques form. Individuals compete for "air time."
- You may be challenged. The team leader may be challenged.
- The purpose of the team may be challenged.

WHAT DOES IT LOOK AND FEEL LIKE?

- Dissatisfaction.
- Hostility.
- Conflict.
- Tension.
- Frustration with each other and with the process.

WHAT SHOULD YOU DO?

- Ask for a frank, orderly expression of opinion.
- Referee disputes and arguments.
- Refocus the team on their task.
- Listen to and paraphrase what different people say.
- Encourage team members to work out their differences.
- Take a deep breath, step back, and let the team resolve its issues.
- Explain that "storming" is a natural part of the team process.
- Assure members that they will get beyond this stage if they are willing to work constructively on their differences.
- Don't ignore the conflict. Don't try to sweep it under a rug. It will come back to haunt you and the team later.

NORMING

The norming stage is a great relief after storming. During norming, the team usually feels closer and more cohesive because members have worked out most of their differences. It is a time that feels good. It often opens up to include social discussions and informal behaviors like snacking, or eating meals, or getting together outside the team sessions.

WHAT'S HAPPENING?

- Team members are beginning to understand each other.
- Members support each other, agreeing about rules, norms and behaviors.
- Members openly disagree about issues instead of criticizing individuals or ideas.
- The team works at maintaining harmonious relationships by talking about fun topics or meeting socially.
- Most work gets done as a team rather than through delegating individual assignments. The team feels a need to do work together.
- Creative ideas are generated.

WHAT DOES IT LOOK AND FEEL LIKE?

- Harmony.
- Cohesion.
- Trust and support.
- Open communication.
- Spontaneity.

WHAT SHOULD YOU DO?

- Continue to model disciplined, creative problem-solving.
- Reinforce the team's positive behaviors.
- Provide focus on the task when the team wants to socialize.
- Give members feedback on their performance.
- Structure personal sharing through a "check-in" technique.
- Challenge the team to think beyond itself—to customer's, other employer's, and management's perspectives.

PERFORMING

The performing stage builds on the positive feeling of the norming stage. The major difference is a shift in focus to being more task oriented. Now the team is willing, ready and able to get the job done.

WHAT IS HAPPENING?

- Focus is on achievement, problems are solved, decisions are made.
- Emphasis is on performance and productivity.
- More tasks may be delegated to individuals because the team no longer feels like it has to do everything together.

WHAT DOES IT LOOK AND FEEL LIKE?

- Intensity.
- Cooperation.
- Interdependence.
- Making progress.

WHAT SHOULD YOU DO?

- Continue to demonstrate confidence in the team.
- Summarize and clarify discussions, decisions, etc.
- Check to determine that the progress is consistent with the task of the team.
- Let the team do the work. Back off. Stop intervening.
- If they need help, give feedback on your observations. Challenge them to figure things out.

ADJOURNING

The adjourning stage is the wrap-up stage for the team. This is the time where people feel a need for recognition, a sense of accomplishment, and closure on the team process.

WHAT IS HAPPENING?

- Assessment of accomplishments.
- Possible resistance to ending the team.
- Team strives for closure and positive reinforcement.
- Celebration and recognition.

WHAT DOES IT LOOK AND FEEL LIKE?

- Uncertainty about the end.
- Appreciation for each other.
- Sadness.
- Desire for recognition.
- Feeling a need to celebrate.

WHAT SHOULD YOU DO?

- Talk about your feelings.
- Hold a "closing event" (dinner, a picnic lunch, party). Get full participation.
- At the event, say a few words about the completed assignment. Have team members share their feelings about the task and the team.
- Find ways to get recognition for the team—company newsletter, annual report, large conference, management meeting, etc.
- Provide team feedback. Be specific!
- Remember: Feedback influences performance, expectations and motivation on future teams.

SUMMARY

By understanding the stages of team development, you will be better able to successfully facilitate a team. The key is to give the team the help that they need as they need it.

Provide structure during forming. Don't overreact during storming. Push a little during norming. Back off during performing. And join in the celebration when adjourning.

Section Two:

DEALING WITH DIFFICULT BEHAVIORS

In any team, there will be times when you have to deal with some kinds of disruptive, difficult, or even dysfunctional behaviors. These are usually individual behaviors, acted out by one person, unlike conflict which is more likely to be acted out between groups or individuals.

SOME EXAMPLES OF DIFFICULT BEHAVIOR:

- Long winded speakers.
- Side conversations.
- Interrupting.
- Silence.
- Off subject speeches.
- Personal attacks.
- Harping on negatives.
- Sleeping.

Let's take a look at an approach using graded interventions for dealing with difficult behavior on teams and in meetings. We'll start with low risk interventions and move on to some with more risk and difficulty.

PREVENTION

Work done before a team convenes and work done during the first team meetings can prevent many problems from ever occurring.

Talk with individual team members before the first team meeting and address problems which you think might occur. Build ground rules at the first meeting to define appropriate team behavior. Remind all team members that they are responsible for upholding and enforcing the team ground rules. Provide training for team members on team skills, problem solving, and meeting skills.

How To's

PREVENT BEHAVIOR PROBLEMS

- Prepare thoroughly for team meetings and projects.
- Practice specific comments you might use to intervene.
- Have solutions prepared before problems arise.
- When you have concerns, discuss them with the individual outside of the team setting.
- Plan seating arrangements so that everyone can see everyone else. Avoid creating "power" positions, like the head of the table or the corner of the room.

NON-INTERVENTION

Usually, when someone is acting in a difficult way, the first step you should take is not to intervene at all. Pause a moment and see if other team members handle the situation. Most of the time, team members will bring others into line by referring to the Ground Rules, or by simply asking them to stop what they are doing.

If the behavior continues, and no one else steps in, you might have to intervene. If the behavior is destructive to the team, like a personal attack, intervene immediately.

Use your judgment about when it is appropriate to intervene. Intervening too frequently can inhibit the team and leave the members too dependent on you.

LOW-LEVEL INTERVENTION

Relatively non-threatening techniques designed to short circuit the difficult behavior will frequently take care of the problem. A reference back to the team ground rules may be all that is needed. Something as simple as a shift in eye contact or asking for input from another team member may stop the behavior.

How To's

MAKE LOW-LEVEL INTERVENTIONS

THE SPEAKER WHO JUST GOES ON AND ON...

- Raise your hand and say, "I'd like to continue."
- Call attention to the agenda and the time line.
- Jump in. Say "thanks." Call on someone else.
- Avoid or break eye contact.

THE MEMBER PLAYING THE "SILENT TYPE"...

- Call on them by name.
- Thank them when they do contribute.
- Establish rapport outside the team setting.
- Use their name.

THERE ARE SIDE CONVERSATIONS...

- Focus the team's attention on something.
- Say, "I'd like to get back on track."
- Say, "Excuse me, I find that distracting."
- Look directly at them and pause.
- Ask if they have something they would like to contribute to the team.

THE INTERRUPTER...

- Enforce the Ground Rules.
- Interrupt the interrupter. Say, "Okay, but let's hear the rest of what John had to say first."
- If it's habitual, take the person aside during a break and discuss the specific behavior that you have observed.

THE RAMBLER...

- Interrupt quickly and firmly.
- Refocus the discussion with a question to another team member or a summary statement.
- Ask direct questions to invite other contributions.

THE CLOWN...

- Ignore.
- Intervene quickly.
- Get control.
- Take a short break if you feel the meeting is out of control.

MEDIUM-LEVEL INTERVENTION

If the behavior is chronic, you may choose to talk with the individual between meetings or at a break. Offer constructive feedback using the guidelines on page 82.

Your goal is to create an informal contract in which the team member agrees to desired behaviors. This may require you to offer certain agreements, too. For example, "I will try to avoid teaming you with Mary on assignments again, but you need to agree to stop arguing with her during the team meetings."

If the team member does not respond to your feedback or suggestions, a more assertive intervention may be called for.

HIGH-LEVEL INTERVENTION

If all else fails, you may have to deal with the offending behavior in the presence of the team.

This is not a step to be taken lightly. A great deal of thought and preparation has to precede such a confrontation.

Avoid blaming. Use constructive feedback and focus on problem solving. Stay focused on the behavior. Keep personalities and stereotypes out of it.

This is a high-risk intervention. It can alienate other team members, even though they may agree with you. It can, however, be very effective.

GIVING CONSTRUCTIVE FEEDBACK

Giving feedback is necessary if teams or individuals are to improve. How it is done will make the difference between an effective intervention and one that turns people off.

When we discuss a problem, people often feel criticized. Not surprisingly, criticism can cause a defensive reaction.

Sometimes even giving praise is not received well.

There are proven ways for giving and receiving feedback, methods that work equally well for giving criticism or praise. These techniques will minimize the likelihood of a defensive reaction on the part of the receiver and will increase the likelihood of effective problem solving.

JUST WHOSE PROBLEM IS IT?

One team member is perpetually late, in spite of a ground rule about starting and ending on time. After weeks of this behavior, you confront the tardy team member.

"I'm sick and tired of you being late all the time! If the rest of us can be here on time, you can too!"

Then you add the giant killer. "I guess you just don't care."

Lateness is an observable, measurable fact. You and the rest of the team observed the lateness through your senses of seeing and hearing.

But using judgmental language, "sick and tired," "late all the time," in describing the behavior, is wrong. The added jab about caring compounds your error. This reflects your interpretation. These are words and phrases that your brain used to describe the sensory data.

Whether the tardy team member cares or not is irrelevant.

Whether you are sick and tired or not is not the issue. And, rarely does anyone do anything all the time.

What you and the team want is everyone to show up on time. You need to focus on the desired behavior rather than try to judge a person's behavior.

Your statement about caring guarantees defensiveness. The rest of your discussion will likely get sidetracked into a debate about caring, which you cannot resolve. You will have lost the entire issue of tardiness and probably alienated a team member.

Whenever facilitators fall into the trap of making interpretations, they have lost a sense of objectivity and fairness in the intervention.

But, it is easy to fall into this trap, so here are some other "interpretations" to avoid.

- "You're just in this for yourself."
- "You're being selfish."
- "You never agree."
- "You're not a team player."
- "You're so negative."

Let's look at how feedback should be given.

KEEP FEEDBACK SPECIFIC. IF WHAT YOU'RE ABOUT TO SAY CAN'T BE DOCUMENTED WITH OBSERVABLE DATA, WAIT UNTIL YOU CAN IDENTIFY THE SPECIFIC BEHAVIOR BEFORE YOU TRY TO CONDUCT THE DISCUSSION.

GUIDELINES FOR GIVING CONSTRUCTIVE FEEDBACK

1. GET PERMISSION.
   In granting permission, the receiver prepares to listen. Stop if permission is not granted. Try to get an agreement for another time.
2. "WHEN YOU..."
   State the facts. Describe observable behavior. Avoid judgment, labeling, and interpretations.
3. "I FEEL..."
   Describe how the behavior affects YOU, how it makes YOU feel.
4. "BECAUSE I..."
   Explain your interpretation of the behavior. This explains why you feel the way you do.
5. PAUSE FOR DISCUSSION, REACTION. YOU MAY BE OFFERED A SOLUTION, IN WHICH CASE YOU DON'T HAVE TO GO ON.
   Give the receiver time to respond.
6. "I WOULD LIKE..."
   Describe the change you are seeking from the other person.
7. "BECAUSE..."
   Explain why you think the change would be helpful.
8. "WHAT DO YOU THINK?"
   Listen to the response. Be willing to consider options. Get agreement on changes.

FEEDBACK CHECKLIST

- Be specific. Use a quote or describe an actual event. Don't use generalities.
- Is this an appropriate time and place for feedback? Feedback should not embarrass either of you.
- Don't be judgmental, avoid labels and interpretations.
- Check to see if you are being heard and understood.
- Empathize with the receiver of the feedback.
- Focus on problem solving. Offer and/or seek ideas to support improvement.
- As improvement occurs, acknowledge it and reinforce it. Use praise and show appreciation for the change in behavior.

POSITIVE FEEDBACK!

So far, we've been discussing things you'd really rather not hear. What about the good stuff? What about giving positive feedback?

Here are a few guidelines for giving positive feedback.

1. MAKE A GENERAL REFERENCE TO THE TOPIC.
   "I wanted to talk to you about how well your presentation to senior management went today."
2. STATE SPECIFICS.
   "It was clear, concise and well organized. You got right to the point and explained the costs and benefits well."
3. MENTION PERSONAL QUALITIES.
   "You're a big-picture thinker and understand issues from other points of view."
4. MENTION THE RESULTS.
   "I just heard from our VP that there's a good chance they'll approve the proposal. Even if they don't, your presentation gave us a lot of credibility."

Doesn't this seem like a compliment that will "stick?" It sure beats that old "Great Job."

RECEIVING FEEDBACK ON YOUR OWN PERFORMANCE

So far, we've been talking about giving feedback.

Now it's time for the tough stuff. Receiving feedback about our own performance. As the facilitator, if you are using the Plan-Do-Study-Act process, you should build in a procedure that allows the team to give you feedback on your own performance.

Here are some guidelines for receiving feedback:

- See the feedback as data. Recognize that it has the potential of helping you improve your performance.
- Listen carefully.
- Seek clarity. Ask for examples. Ask questions.

If what you are getting is their interpretation or a generalization of what they saw or heard that made them think the way they do.

- Acknowledge the feedback.
- Ask for solutions.
- Reflect on the feedback you've been given. Identify the points which seem valid.
- If appropriate, contract for change. You can make this contract with yourself, or with the team that gave you the feedback.

Section Four:

DEALING WITH CONFLICT

As we discussed in the Stages of Team Development, you can expect to have to deal with some conflict as a normal part of your assignment. Conflict is not necessarily a bad thing.

There can be benefits to having conflict emerge on a team. It can challenge assumptions, allow frustrations to get aired, bring simmering hostility to the surface, and it can force the team to resolve difficult issues. Conflict can even serve to energize the team.

Your challenge is to manage the conflict so that the benefits do occur. You need to remain objective and impartial. You cannot become a participant in the conflict. It is essential to maintain your position as an impartial and fair moderator for the team.

Remember: Conflict will continue if individuals feel ignored or misunderstood. Let team members know that they have been heard by paraphrasing and summarizing all points of view. Check with them to be certain that your restatement is accurate from their point of view.

How To's

FACILITATE CONFLICT

- Enforce appropriate ground rules that the team has established.
- Summarize the points of view being expressed.
- Ask individuals to summarize the other party's point of view.
- Indicate your desire to have the team listen to and understand the different points of view.
- Intervene immediately if the conflict turns into personal attack.
- Contact specific team members between meetings for individual discussion and clarification.
- Time out. Be willing to call a break if you need time to plan your conflict intervention or to let people cool down.
- Try a force fit. Ask team members to take an idea they disagree with and modify it to make it work.
- Ask team members to identify the core value in their argument. Ask if they think the team is missing this point.
- Praise working through conflict. Admit that this creates tension, but emphasize its value in gaining a thorough examination of ideas.

What If?

WHAT IF... A TEAM MEMBER "LOSES IT"...?

- Don't take sides.
- Maintain everyone's self-esteem.
- Don't get emotional.
- Refocus on the objective.
- Adjourn the meeting, or take a break.

WHAT IF... TEAM MEMBERS DON'T LIKE EACH OTHER?

- Discuss your perceptions with the team keeping the discussion based on observed behavior.
- Ask each faction what they would like the "other" to do differently and what they are willing to do themselves to make the situation better.
- Remind the group that, no matter how painful, the situation will improve just by talking about it.

WHAT IF .... ARGUMENTS BREAK OUT?

- Move the discussion away from personalities and back to the actual problem.
- Try rephrasing the comments into general questions to the team.
- Discourage a back-and-forth exchange between the two people. Draw others, especially those who seem neutral, into the discussion.
- Ask the rest of the group to comment on the exchange.
- Restate the issue. Try to clarify it while giving everyone some breathing space in the fast-paced discussion.
- Ask the opponents to summarize each other's position. Sometimes simple misunderstandings are the basis of the argument. Re-statement of the other's argument can lead to clarity and peace.

Remember: Your objective is to stop the one-on-one interchange without losing the valuable insights that argument often brings to problem solving. Keep the focus on the issues. Don't hide from strong feelings. Use them to illuminate the issue.

CHAPTER 5

NINE STEPS

A TEMPLATE FOR YOUR NEXT TEAM MEETING

The purpose of this last chapter is to give you a quick outline for facilitating an effective team. This can serve as a reminder. Or, it can serve as your template. Ready? Let's get going.

STEP ONE: YOUR ROLE

- Work with the Team Leader.
- Plan the first meeting together.
- Focus on the process not the content.
- Provide directions and tools that improve the process.
- Give feedback to the team and to individuals.
- Evaluate the team's process.
- Work with the team on improvements.
- Be objective. Stay neutral on the task.
- Summarize and paraphrase what you hear in the meetings.
- Do not dominate or try to control the team. Manage the process.
- Challenge the team to listen to and consider all ideas and perspectives.

STEP TWO: MEETING MANAGEMENT

PLAN

- Agenda.
- Objectives.
- Timing.
- Logistics.
- Ground Rules.

DO

- Icebreakers or check-in.
- Review Ground Rules.
- Involve everyone.
- Keep notes and records.
- Keep the team focused.
- Summarize and paraphrase.

STUDY

- Is the team accomplishing its goals?
- Is the team working together?
- How is the Team Leader performing?
- How are you performing?

ACT

- Change the process based on feedback.
- Plan next agenda during the current meeting.
- Implement the team's recommendations.

STEP THREE: THE FIRST MEETING

1. Meet with the Team Leader to create an agenda.
2. Send the agenda to team members.
3. Introductions. Ask everyone to say who they are, what they do, and why they are on the team.
4. Icebreaker. Get everyone loose from the start.
5. Clarify the Goal or Mission of the team.
6. Get the team to build a set of Ground Rules to regulate performance.
7. Review the process you and the team will use to achieve its goal.
8. Discuss logistics, schedules, and the time and place for the next meeting.
9. Work together to build the agenda for the next meeting.
10. Explain your role in the process. Clarify any misunderstandings.
11. Check-out, ask for feedback or evaluations of the meeting, the team, and the goal.

STEP FOUR: DEFINE THE PROBLEM

If you want to define the problem, have the team find answers to these questions.

Q 1. What, exactly, is the problem?

Q 2. How do we know that it is a problem?

Q 3. What data or information do we have about this problem?

Q 4. Who are the key players in the organization with regards to this problem?

Q 5. What is their perspective?

Q 6. What is the root cause?

Q 7. Is there other data or information that could help us understand the problem?

Q 8. How will we know when we have solved the problem?

STEP FIVE: GENERATING CREATIVE IDEAS

- Remind team members to think like “artists” rather than “judges.”
- Use a variety of techniques:
  - Brainstorming
  - Brainwriting
  - Forced Relationships
  - Affinity Process

- Maintain a positive environment by enforcing the Ground Rules.
- Encourage wild and zany ideas.
- On occasion, change the setting for the meeting to eliminate distractions and encourage relaxation.
- Be certain to record all ideas.
- Provoke the "quiet" ones.
- Use a round-robin technique during brainstorming if necessary to keep participation balanced.

STEP SIX: DECISION MAKING

- The team has reached a consensus when everyone agrees to support the decision.
- Multi-voting can reduce the number of ideas under consideration to a manageable few for serious discussion.
- Work with the team to build the criteria you will use to evaluate the different options.
- A Decision Matrix can be used to evaluate ideas against criteria.
- Summarize and paraphrase frequently. Broad agreement and common understanding are critical to decision making.
- Test for consensus by asking if proposed decisions have support and approval from every member of the team.

STEP SEVEN: PREVENTING PEOPLE PROBLEMS

- Build and use the Ground Rules.
- Set and keep a positive tone.
- Regularly clarify expectations and roles.
- Strive for balanced participation.
- Let the team evaluate the process.
- Let the team evaluate you.
- Secure or provide training in team skills for team members.
- Help the Team Leader seek and attract motivated people for the team.

STEP EIGHT: DEALING WITH CONFLICT

- Enforce the Ground Rules.
- Make sure that everyone gets listened to.
- Remind the team that conflict can be positive.
- Use "time-outs" when necessary.
- Summarize objectively.
- Talk to conflicting parties outside the team setting.
- Seek outside support for breaking deadlocks.
- Keep the team focused on its goals.
- Keep the team aimed at consensus.

STEP NINE: IMPLEMENTATION

- Help the team plan for the changes it is proposing.
- Plan for:
  - Acceptance
  - Necessary resources
  - Timing
  - Communication
  - Contingencies
  - Momentum
- Force Field Analysis can help to identify resources, problems, and opportunities.
- Troll Search is powerful in identifying and labeling the fears about change.
- Involve the affected people in planning for change.
- Communicate.
- Remember "Plan-Do-Study-Act," the model works here, too.
  - Plan the change.
  - Do the change (The team might propose a pilot project first.)
  - Study the change (What works? What doesn't?)
  - Act on the feedback to improve the change.

What If? INDEX

What If... | *Page*

How To's INDEX

KEY WORD INDEX

HOWICK ASSOCIATES

Since the first day of business in 1984, Howick Associates has concentrated on providing human resource solutions through consulting and training services. The company has worked with more than four hundred organizations ranging in size from huge multi-nationals to small non-profits. Howick Associates has earned a reputation among clients as a provider of services "tailored" to their specific needs.

Consulting services cover the broad spectrum of human resource issues including management assessments, management succession planning, workplace evaluations, employee surveys, sales and marketing force development, employee development systems, implementing quality improvement throughout an organization, and stakeholder involvement issues. Training programs are developed around five core competencies: Communications Skills, Team Building and Development, Quality Improvement, Leadership and Management Development, and Career Planning.

Howick Associates works to create a partnership with its clients so that the team developing solutions to the client's problems involves participants from both organizations.

In addition, Howick Associates provides frequent forums for clients and client groups to meet to discuss emerging topics in the human resource field. These sessions, which combine aspects of focus group research and informal feedback meetings, may result in new products and services for the profession. The Compleat Facilitator package grew out of a series of such sessions.

Human Resource Solutions Since 1984

ORDER TODAY!

YES!
Send me The Compleat Facilitator: A Guide

Send to:

Name ______________________________

Organization ______________________________

____

Title ______________________________

Address ______________________________

City__________ State______ Zip __________

Phone (_____) ______________________________

ORDER FORM

The Compleat Facilitator: A Guide $29.95

Quantity

_____ 1-10 copies ($29.95 each) __________
_____ 11-24 copies ($25.45 each) __________
_____ 25 or more ($21.95 each) __________
WI Sales Tax (5%) __________

Postage and Handling

1 copy add $3.65 __________
for each add'l add $1.35 __________

*Note: for orders of more than 25 copies, HOWICK ASSOCIATES will pay the postage and handling.

Total enclosed: __________

Payment: ☐ Check enclosed ☐ VISA ☐ MasterCard Card # __________ Exp. Date __________

Card Holder's Signature ______________________________

Mail to: HOWICK ASSOCIATES • 2828 Marshall Court, Suite 100 • Madison, WI 53705 • FAX: 608-233-1194

ORDER TODAY!

YES!
Send me The Compleat Facilitator: A Guide

Send to:

Name ______________________________

Organization ______________________________

____

Title ______________________________

Address ______________________________

City__________ State______ Zip __________

Phone (_____) ______________________________

ORDER FORM

The Compleat Facilitator: A Guide $29.95

Quantity

_____ 1-10 copies ($29.95 each) __________
_____ 11-24 copies ($25.45 each) __________
_____ 25 or more ($21.95 each) __________
WI Sales Tax (5%) __________

Postage and Handling

1 copy add $3.65 __________
for each add'l add $1.35 __________

*Note: for orders of more than 25 copies, HOWICK ASSOCIATES will pay the postage and handling.

Total enclosed: __________

Payment: ☐ Check enclosed ☐ VISA ☐ MasterCard Card # __________ Exp. Date __________

Card Holder's Signature ______________________________

Mail to: HOWICK ASSOCIATES • 2828 Marshall Court, Suite 100 • Madison, WI 53705 • FAX: 608-233-1194

ORDER TODAY!

YES!
Send me The Compleat Facilitator: A Guide

Send to:

Name ______________________________

Organization ______________________________

____

Title ______________________________

Address ______________________________

City__________ State______ Zip __________

Phone (_____) ______________________________

ORDER FORM

The Compleat Facilitator: A Guide $29.95

Quantity

_____ 1-10 copies ($29.95 each) __________
_____ 11-24 copies ($25.45 each) __________
_____ 25 or more ($21.95 each) __________
WI Sales Tax (5%) __________

Postage and Handling

1 copy add $3.65 __________
for each add'l add $1.35 __________

*Note: for orders of more than 25 copies, HOWICK ASSOCIATES will pay the postage and handling.

Total enclosed: __________

Payment: ☐ Check enclosed ☐ VISA ☐ MasterCard Card # __________ Exp. Date __________

Card Holder's Signature ______________________________

Mail to: HOWICK ASSOCIATES • 2828 Marshall Court, Suite 100 • Madison, WI 53705 • FAX: 608-233-1194